Everyday Chamorro

M.B. Dallocchio

The Desert Institute

Las Vegas, Nevada

ISBN: 0692404333
ISBN-13: 978-0692404331
Printed in the United States of America

The Desert Institute
www.desert-institute.org

CONTENTS

INTRODUCTION

Despite numerous claims of links to other languages, modern Chamorro is a hispanicized Austronesian language indigenous to the Mariana Islands (primarily Guam, Saipan, Tinian, and Rota). The indigenous Austronesian aspect of the language still exists, however due to various visitors and occupants; the language is now colored in Asian and Anglo words in addition to the obvious Spanish roots.

Chamorros are Pacific Islanders and more specifically, Micronesian. Not Asian. Asians and Pacific Islanders are not racially identical, they are two separate ethnic groups. Chamorros migrated thousands of years ago from Asia as did Native Americans, who have a separate racial category and cultural identity as well.

Maintaining one's identity through colonialism and imperialism is vital in keeping the Chamorro language and culture alive. Additionally, languages stemming from Indonesia to Easter Island have a few words in common and even some stems, but some are more closely linked than others. If you examine ancient Chamorro numbers, you will find some words are closer to Samoan rather than any other Southeast Asian language. Chamorros were the first to cross into the Pacific over 7000 years ago and some of the ancient traditions are being revived today in order to pass on the cultural riches and language to our descendants for generations to come.

In hopes of preserving the Chamorro language, this book is designed to get you started in using everyday phrases in Chamorro. While it will take much more than this book to help you to become fluent, I hope that you enjoy this book and that it serves to be a helpful guide in speaking Chamorro on a daily basis.

1 GETTING DOWN TO THE BASICS

Hafa adai!
Hello!

How to Learn a Language

Learning a language isn't an easy task, even if you are the type who's more linguistically inclined. However, when one is learning a rare language such as Chamorro, studying can be extremely intimidating. Chamorro language materials are sparse at best and there are quite a few people out there sending mixed messages on Chamorro spelling, grammar, and pronunciation. So anyone who is seriously taking on Chamorro with the goal of fluency or at least near-fluency deserves a great big pat on the back.

Whether you're learning Chamorro because it's part of your heritage, for pure polyglot curiosity, or just to learn a few phrases to be a polite visitor to the Marianas, below you'll find a few pointers to help you get started. This compilation is a list of ways to keep your Chamorro language learning on track in order to achieve your language acquisition goals.

How to Learn a Language: Chamorro Style

1. Be Realistic in Setting Your Language Goals

Be honest with yourself. How much do you really want to learn? Whether you want to learn Chamorro for your family or just for fun, you should set a goal for yourself according to what level you want to reach. You may wonder how long it might take you to learn Chamorro on a basic, intermediate, or advanced-fluent level, but, in reality, that's entirely up to you. However, if you remain dedicated and committed to the language learning process, giving yourself a year at a time for each of the three stages is completely feasible.

If you're starting at a basic level, give yourself a year to learn grammar, sentence structure and basic vocabulary. Basic level students will often make mistakes and this is perfectly normal. This level of proficiency indicates that the person will find it extremely difficult to carry on in a conversation without rehearsed material. One might ask, how will one know if they're truly advancing in a language even at the basic level? One good indicator is that you'll start to dream in the language. So when you start using Chamorro in your dream dialogues, you'll know you're getting somewhere, and take note of it!

At an intermediate level, one should be able to be able to handle casual conversations, yet with some errors, and be able to describe oneself and surroundings with little to no difficulty. At this level, one needs guidance but not frequently. Accent and pronunciation should be understandable, but there still may be flaws at this stage. Grammar and sentence structure are understood at this level in speaking, reading and writing.

At an advanced level, you should be fully confident in everything you've learned at the intermediate level and ready to handle yourself in all aspects of communicating in Chamorro. One should be at the level below that of a fully fluent and articulate native speaker. An advanced level speaker may still have occasional mistakes when it comes to Chamorro idioms and/or colloquialisms.

And of course, fluent is the highest point where one could reach in Chamorro as in any other language. One should have fulfilled the criteria of the advanced level and be able to handle themselves in any social situation along with demonstrated proficiency in reading and writing.

2. Choose What Interests You Most and Go For It

Whether it's profanity, tourism, talking to grandparents, history, preservation or any other personal reason for learning Chamorro, start with what you like. Think about what you want to know how to say regarding your interests. For example, if you want to speak with elder Chamorro relatives, one might want to be able to start a conversation and ask the person questions i.e. "Is there anything I can do for you?", "In which village were you born?", "What was Saipan like during WWII?" Anything. Write your list out and get going on a quest to get it translated into Chamorro. You can ask a native speaker or start with Chamorro dictionaries, but try looking up words on your own first.

3. Create A Study Plan and Style

What kind of learner are you? Do you remember things better by hearing a recording or do you need to write things down? Get a recorder, a notebook, anything to help you out, but for starters, a simple notepad at first will help you get motivated and ready to write wherever you go. Figure out your favorite method to keep track of your language progress and stick to it, but bear in mind that you need to be able to speak, listen, read, and write in Chamorro to be fully fluent.

If you're not sure where to begin, the best way to get started for the long-haul is with index cards and/or a notebook. Get yourself organized through creating tabs or folders for grammar, vocabulary, phrases, and extra paper to practice dictation. Consolidate your materials exclusively for Chamorro language learning and get started on your lists.

4. If Possible, Find a Tutor

One might not think about it, but if you live in the Marianas, particularly the Commonwealth of the Northern Mariana Islands (CNMI), you should not be experiencing a shortage in access to conversing with fluent speakers. Ask someone to be a tutor and of course, offer something in return whether it be monetary gift or a trade. A tutor is your walking dictionary, but make sure they're a native, fluent speaker. You don't have to hang around this person all day, every day, but the more exposure to Chamorro you have, even when you don't completely understand the conversation, the better for your future comprehension. Try to make an arrangement of a couple hours per week or more if time permits for you or the native speaker.

5. Cheat Sheets and List-Making

Everywhere you go, you want to be able to pull out your lists or note cards whenever possible. Instead of playing with your cell phone or twiddling your thumbs, practicing your Chamorro is the cure for your boredom if you're a committed student. Whatever you're trying to learn, whether it's phrases or a vocabulary list, make it accessible at all times until you've mastered it.

6. Adopt the "Parrot Attitude"

Listen closely to Chamorro conversations and imitate the sounds and words in your mind. If possible, record your own voice and try to point out what you need to improve. Imitate the accent - obviously not in front of the people you're listening to - and pay close attention to which words tend to be used the most and which words you're not sure of.

7. Repetition-Repetition-Repetition

It's boring, but it helps. It's not enough to know a few songs or a hymn. You may even try saying the rosary in Chamorro. There are plenty of old words, it's all in Chamorro, and there is plenty of repetition. If you can do this on your own, and without looking at a book or a cheat sheet, you're definitely on the intermediate level and on your way to the advanced level of Chamorro language learning. Repetition, association, and mnemonic devices will definitely help you in vocabulary retention.

8. Stay Disciplined

Falling off the language wagon is usually a cause for not advancing in this area of study. One day you're enthusiastic, ready to take on the language world and another day, it just seems to be overwhelming. Stay disciplined. Language learning isn't easy, but if you really want to achieve a certain level of proficiency, make language practice a daily task.

9. Humility

Feeling uneasy, embarrassed, making numerous mistakes, and getting laughed at certainly isn't a great feeling, but guess what? Everyone who learns a second, third, or fourth language goes through the same process of humiliation. It is a linguistic rite of passage. Therefore, it takes humility to put your ego aside and place yourself in awkward situations. Force yourself to speak Chamorro whenever the opportunity presents itself.

10. Keep Setting New Goals and Never Stop Learning

There is no zenith in learning a language, but being able to communicate fluently should be your goal. Even when you are at the fluent stage, there are probably words you still won't know. And that's fine, so long as you strive to learn more words and perfect your communication in Chamorro. Keep setting goals for yourself and once you reach them, create more goals, and never stop learning.

PRONUNCIATION GUIDE

In Chamorro, you have to be careful with pronunciation as vowels are not always the same, but there are a few that remain constant:

a 'ah' as in 'father' or 'a' as in 'cat'

note: å is not used in original Chamorro orthography as indicated by the Marianas Orthography Committee since 1971. The letter å is more commonly used in Guamanian dialect and is a fairly new concept. It is unoriginal to the Chamorro language and while it may help some in reading vowel pronunciation, it is not consistent and will not be used in this book.

e 'eh' as in 'bend' or 'ee' as in 'feet'

i 'ee' as in 'feet'

o 'oh' as in vote or 'oo' as in 'food'

u 'oo' as in 'food'

y is pronounced as 'dz' as in the 'ds' in 'kids'

ch 'ch' as in 'cheese' or 'ts' as in 'tsunami'

j 'h' as in 'hello'; there are very few Chamorro words with 'j'

ñ 'ny' as in 'canyon'

The remainder of consonants in the chamorro alphabet:

b 'b' as in 'branch'

d 'd' as in 'double'

f 'f' as in 'fox'

g 'g' as in 'go'

h 'h' as in 'hotel'

k 'k' as in 'kid'

l 'l' as in 'little'

m 'm' as in 'mint'

n 'n' as in 'night'

p 'p' as in 'pen'

r 'r' as in 'red'

s 's' as in 'sign'

t 't' as in 'tango'

Everyday Expressions

Welcome - **Bienbenidu**
Hello - **Hafa Adai**
Hi - **Buenas**
Good morning - **Buenos dihas**
Good afternoon - **Buenos tatdes**
Good evening - **Buenas noches**
Yes – **Hunggan/Hu'u/ A'a**
No – **Ahe'**
Please – **Pot Fabot**
Thank you – **Si Yu'us ma'ase** or **Saina ma'ase**
You're welcome - **Buen prubechu**
Excuse me/Sorry - **Dispensa yu**
Please excuse me - **Dispensa-yu, pot fabot**
It doesn't matter - **Taya guaha**
It's all right - **Maolek ha**
Good-bye – **Adios**
Until tomorrow - **Esta agupa**
Until we meet again - **Estaki manali'e hit ta'lo**
See you later - **Ta a'ali'e despues**

How are you? - **Hafa tatamanu hao?** / **Hafa mamaoleka?**
I'm fine - **Maolek ha' yu** / **Todo maolek**
Long time no see - **Apmam tiempo ti uli'e hao**

What's your name? - **Hayi na'an-mu?**
My name is ... - **Na'an-hu si...**

Where are you from? - **Taotao manu hao?**
I'm from ... - **Taotao ... yu**
Pleased to meet you - **Ma'gof yu sa umali'i hit**

Hi, friend - **Hafa lai/ga'chong/che'lu**
How are you? - **Hafa tatamanu hao? Hafa mamaoleka?**
Fine, and you? – **Maolek, yan hagu?**
I'm fine too - **Maolek lokkue**
Come in – **Maila halom**
How is your family? - **Hafa manatatamanu i familia-mu?**

They are not so good - **Ti man gof maolek**

They are fine. And your family?
Manmamaolek ha'. Yan i familia-mu?

They are fine too.
Manmamaolek ha' lokkue.

Come and visit us at home when you have time.
Fanmambisisita guatu gi gima yanggen guaha lugat-miyu.

Alright, if we have time.
Po'lu na'i ya yanggen guaha lugat.

You too, come and visit us. - **Hamyo lokkue, fanmambisita.**

Ok. Thank you. Bye - **Esta. Si yu'us ma'ase. Adios**
Good-bye - **Adios**
Good-bye, friend - **Adios, ga'chong**
Until we see each other again - **Estaki manali'e hit ta'lo**
Until tomorrow - **Esta agupa**
See you later - **Ta a'ali'e despues**
Good luck! - **Suette!**
Cheers/Good health! - **Hago lao!**
Have a nice day - **Puedi ha todo maolek**
Bon appetit - **Buen prubechu**
Bon voyage - **Buen biahe**

How much is this? - **Kuanto baliña este?**
Where is the…? - **Mangge i…?**

Where is the restroom?
Mangge i kemmon?/ Manu na gaige i kemmon?

Numbers

Ordinal Numbers

1st	Finene'na
2nd	I mina dos
3rd	I mina tres
4th	I mina kuattro
5th	I mina sinko
6th	I mina sais
7th	I mina sette
8th	I mina ocho
9th	I mina nuebe
10th	I mina dies

1	Uno	21	Beinte Uno
2	Dos	30	Trenta
3	Tres	40	Kuarenta
4	Kuatro	50	Sinkuenta
5	Sinko	60	Sesenta
6	Sais	70	Setenta
7	Siete	80	Ochenta
8	Ocho	90	Nobenta
9	Nuebe	100	Siento
10	Dies	101	Siento Uno
11	Onse	200	Dosientos...
12	Dose	500	Kinientos
13	Trese	600	Saisientos...
14	Katotse		
15	Kinse		
16	Diesisais	1,000	Mit
17	Diesisiete	10,000	Dies Mit
18	Diesiocho	100,000	Sien Mit
19	Diesinuebe	1,000,000	Un Miyon
20	Beinte	1,000,000,000	Biyon

Shapes

circle – **sitkolo**
diamond – **diamante**
heart – **korason**
half circle – **medio sitkolo**
oval – **adamelong/ubulao**
rectangle – **rektanggolo**
round – **aridondo**
square – **kuadrao**
star – **estreya**
triangle – **trianggolo**

Colors

black – **attelong**
blue – **asut**
brown – **kulot chukulati**
gray – **kulot apu**
green – **betde**
gold – **kulot oru**
orange – **kulot kahet**
pink – **kulot di rosa**
purple – **lila**
red – **agaga'**
silver – **kulot salappe'**
tan – **kulot kueru**
yellow – **amariyu**
white – **a'paka'**

Days, Months, and Time

pre-dawn – **chatangmak**
dawn – **machakchak kattan**
morning star – **luseru**
sunrise – **kinahulo' atdao**
early morning – **pa'go manana**
morning - **ogga'an**
pre-noon, noon, past noon – **talo'ani**
day - **ha'ani**
sunset – **minachom atdao**
late afternoon, early evening – **pupuengi**
night – **puengi**
midnight – **tatalo' puengi**

early – **taftaf**
late – **atrasao**

yesterday – **nigap**
today – **pa'go**
tomorrow – **agupa**

day – **diha/dia**
month – **mes**
year – **sakkan/año**
season – **sakkan/tiempo**

Dry season – **Tiempon somnak, Fañomnagan**
Rainy season – **Tiempon uchan, Fanuchanan**

The Mariana Islands has consistently warm weather, so there is not a great degree in temperature change regardless of the season. The rainy season begins in August and ends in mid-January, which is why it's associated with typhoon season. From mid-January through July is the dry season.

A Note on the Calendar System

Prior to Spanish colonization in the 1500's, Chamorros had a 13-month calendar system, the extra month appearing in mid-December. The Chamorro calendar was based on a 13-month lunar cycle with specific marine and weather indicators, much like Samoa and other Pacific Island cultures. Below is a chart that shows the old Chamorro months and the modern Spanish conversion.

English	Modern Chamorro	Ancient Chamorro	Meaning	Constellation/Star
January	Eneru	Tumaiguini	Like this	Corona Borealis
February	Febreru	Maimo	(no translation)	
March	Matsu	Umatalaf	To catch gatafe fish	Altair
April	Abrit	Lumuhu	To go back	
May	Mayu	Makmamao	(no translation)	Aries
June	Junio	Mananaf	The crawling time	
July	Julio	Semo	(no translation)	Aldebaran
August	Agosto	Tenhos	Angry	Orion's belt
September	Septembre	Lumamlam	Lightning	Sirius
October	Oktubre	Fanggualo'	Planting time	Corvus
November	Nobiembre	Sumongsong	To put in the stopper	Arcturus
December	Disiembre	Umayanggan	Troubled melancholy	Antares
		Umagahaf	To get crawfish	

Days of the Week	Months of the Year
	Eneru - **January**
Monday – **Lunes**	Febreru - **February**
Tuesday – **Mattes**	Matso - **March**
Wednesday – **Metkoles**	Abrit - **April**
Thursday – **Huebes**	Mayu - **May**
Friday – **Betnes**	Hunio - **June**
Saturday – **Sabalu**	Hulio - **July**
Sunday – **Damenggo**	Agostu - **August**
	Settembre - **September**
	Oktubre - **October**
	Nobiembre - **November**
	Disiembre - **December**

What time is it? - **Ki ora esta?**
What time is it there? **Ki ora guenao?**
It's time - **Esta ora**
It's one o'clock. It's two o'clock. **Oran ala una. Oran alas dos.**

Hafa taimanu un sangan…?
How do you say…?

Kao siña hu ayuda hao?
May I help you?

Kao siña hao fumino' Chamorro?
Do you speak Chamorro?

A'a, didide' ha.
Yes, a little.

Yanggen ti un lalalo', kao siña un ayuda yu?
If you don't mind, can you help me?

Hu nisisita didide' na ayudu.
I need a little help.

Hafa taimanu un sangan _____ gi fino' Chamorro?
How do you say _____ in Chamorro?

Ti hu kumprende.
I don't understand.

Pot fabot na despasio i kuentos-mu.
Please speak more slowly.

Tuge' papa pot fabot.
Please write it down.

Hu gof agradesi i inayuda-mu.
I really appreciate your help.

2 CUSTOMS AND CULTURE

Mangginge'
Showing respect to the elders

In Chamorro culture, it is customary to greet elders by kissing the top of their hand and asking for a blessing which is called **Mangginge'** or **Amen**. At Chamorro events you may hear a parent tell their child to "Go *amen*" an aunt, uncle, or whomever is present and is an elder to the child. This is done for those who are parents, aunts, uncles, and older.

More specifically, when **mangginge'** is done, you say "Ñot" or "Ñora," which is actually short for the Spanish *Señor* and *Señora*. This is to show respect and in return, the elder may nod, make the sign of the cross on you, or may even say "**Para bai hu tayuyuti hao**," which means "I'll pray for you." The kissing on the hand is not necessarily a kiss with puckered lips onto the hand, but done in a way that you gently bite down on both of your lips so that they aren't showing and inhale the elders hand, so as to inhale their spirit and wisdom.

Ñot – what you say when you 'amen' a man
Ñora – what you say when you 'amen' a woman
Respetu – Respect

Ayuda – Help
Guinaiya – Love
Inadahi – Care
Ina'fa'maolek – to make good with each other, make peace
Konsiderasion – Consideration
Pas – Peace

Linaknos/Lina'los - contribution or donation
Ika - gift for sad occasions, i.e. funeral
Chenchule' - gift for happy occasions i.e. wedding

The difference between being a Suruhana, Le'an, and using Atgimat

The topics of **Suruhanu/a**'s, being **le'an**, and **atgimat** aren't unfamiliar terms to those who have been raised with Chamorro culture, and it is something that can be easily misunderstood by outsiders. Divination, traditional medicine, and shamanism are often immediately connected to "witchcraft." This is a common misconception by those who typically do not know what they're doing (i.e. learning divination and "spells" through reading books and watching movies on the subject). Whether you've got a natural ability, an inclination towards the occult, or plain skepticism, the following is just for cultural information purposes only as Chamorro spirituality can be quite complex.

Suruhanu's and **Suruhana**'s are not witches, warlocks, druids, satanists, sorcerers, witch doctors, vampires, or anything of the sort. Medicine men/medicine women would most likely be the closest English translation in terms of description as being a **Suruhanu** is a specific role that involves extensive family guidance. **Suruhanu's** don't tend to specialize in **kahkana** or black magic, contrary to popular belief by outsiders looking in. Rather, these medicine people specialize in natural remedies and if you're lucky, they might even be **le'an** too. These abilities have to come through family in terms of medicine knowledge and the inherited ability to see spirits, a person's soul, and sometimes even the future.

These things are generally not taught to just anyone or even someone who is interested in learning. These traditions are passed down through families and it's not intended to be merely exclusive, you just have to know the person learning very well to ensure a clear conscience and good intentions. There are not specific rituals to become a **suruhana**, but to become a different type of "practitioner" who engages in curses and other means that interfere with others' lives, there is a certain rite of passage called **ha'ilas** which I'll discuss in the **atgimat** section. **Atgimat** is not a practice that is smiled upon, not because of silly labels, but for interfering directly in people's lives through spells, potions, and other unnatural means of involving yourself in another person's life. Although some practicing **suruhana's** on Saipan are friends with those who go the **ha'ilas** route, it is important to note that both types of people may mix these practices with Roman Catholicism. This is not only due to Spanish influence and tradition, but it is meant for personal protection from harmful spirits either seeking to prevent one from doing good or binding themselves to people involved in **kahkana**. Although the **ha'ilas** route is not as desirable for its interference and spells, you tend to not see judgment between the two different practitioners. A big difference between those of European/Western descent who practice natural healing or witchcraft who do tend to judge one another.

Le'an is a term that is used in Chamorro to identify "psychic" capabilities. This is a separate topic from reading tarot cards and gazing into a crystal ball in case you were wondering. Usually someone who is le'an can have various abilities such as looking at a person and seeing their personality and/or future, seeing spirits or sensing their presence, and other clairvoyant abilities. Being **le'an** is believed to be an inherited trait and not something you can acquire or develop if you don't already have a small amount of this capacity. Sorry, no books about clairvoyance or invoking spirits can make you **le'an**.

Atgimat is still something that is still around and working as people still pay good money for this. In Lawrence Cunningham's "Ancient Chamorro Society", he discusses the use of **kahkana** where casting a spell on someone consisted of taking a part of their body, whether it be hair or feces and mixing it with a concoction sure to make the person ill, afflicted with bad luck, or die a sooner death. Nowadays with centuries of Catholicism mixed with modern Chamorro culture, it is viewed as an unforgivable sin to take part in using atgimat or practicing **kahkana**.

While many westerners tend to view making a deal with the devil or selling your soul as meeting some guy with a pointed tail, horns, and a pitchfork ready to get you to seal your fate on parchment paper with blood ink, this is not the case with Chamorros. Sealing your fate for an afterlife of suffering has more to do with grudges or personally cursing someone through **kahkana**. Whether it's for "love" (or, more accurately, lust) or hate, one should never interfere with another person's will.

Ways to protect oneself, as evident through religious influence, is to be a person of prayer and meditation. If someone lacks spiritual discipline, they put themselves at risk and are vulnerable to curses. Love potions, **atgimat**, are the more commonly purchased items in the Marianas by various groups looking to capture the attention of their object of desire, permanently. This usually runs a person about $300, the standard price for tricking your crush into unconditional adoration, but there is a great downside. Reportedly, if this potion works, the bewitched person will reportedly have difficulty maintaining eye contact with close loved ones and friends prior to the curse and in a few years the curse has to be repeated or else it will wear off and a reverse of the potion will take place, leaving the atgimat victim full of contempt for the love-sick perpetrator. **Atgimat** is administered much like the ancient Chamorro/Micronesian way of getting the target person's hair, nail clippings, or excrements and mixed with the potion or one can slip the potion into someone's food or drink.

As mentioned before, those who have gone through the **ha'ilas** process provide this service. But not all practitioners focus on these interfering spells or rites. Some actually do a half-and-half with **kahkana** and regular **suruhana amot**. Yet whether it's an herbalist, an atgimat enthusiast, someone who is **le'an**, or a combination of sorts, these three different and seemingly supernatural categories are good at identifying if you are gifted or cursed. The last thing you ever want to hear is **"Makahnayi hao!"**

Bukabulariu / Vocabulary:

Amot - Medicine
Atgimat - Curse, love potion/spell
Ha'ilas - Ceremony used in various capacities, sometimes for spiritual cleansing or inititation
Kahnayi – Hex, to curse, bewitch
Kahkana - Black magic, one who performs black magic

Le'an - Naturally gifted in psychic/clairvoyant ability
Lommok - Pestle
Lusong - Mortar

Makahnayi hao.
You've been cursed; Someone put a spell on you.

Suruhana - Healer (f)
Suruhanu - Healer (m)

Chamorro Paranormal Activity

Taotaomo'na – (Lit: People of the past) Taotaomo'na are ancient spirits that tend to dwell around latte stones, nunu (banyan) trees and other parts of the jungle. Often taking on the form of a large, strong male presence, it is said that Taotaomo'na can either be helpful or become angry and cause harm.

In cases where a Taotaomo'na is helpful, or is partnered with a living Chamorro, they are said to increase physical strength and provide other abilities. A suruhana or suruhanu may sometimes be able to communicate with Taotaomo'na depending on their own capabilities (if they are le'an or restricted to herbal healing), and Chamorro prayers must be said to either avoid angering them or to ask for forgiveness of any offense.

Some examples of an offense would include confronting the Taotaomo'na in the Chamorro language, taking fruit or other items from a tree without asking for their permission, desecrating sacred sites, and making excessive noise outdoors at night.

Duendes – Duendes are known as trolls or elf-like beings that hide or deceive children. If mushrooms appear on one's lawn, it is said that duendes were playing around your home. If someone comes into contact with any duendes, a suruhana or suruhanu should be contacted.

White Lady – The legend of the white lady tends to revolve around a story of a woman who is waiting for her spouse or fiancé – who never arrived due to an abrupt death. She is said to be seen around bridges, waiting around water, or walking around alone at night. The white lady is completely clothed in white, is very beautiful, and is often accompanied with the scent of ylang ylang or roses. She is an omen of bad luck or is said to make others sick.

Prefixes and Suffixes

In the Chamorro language, there are a certain amount of letters attached to the beginnings and ends of words depending upon what the speaker is attempting to communicate. Conjugation and tenses are found within these prefixes and suffixes as opposed to being mere root words as in other languages. So if you're studying Chamorro for the first time or just brushing up on your speaking, reading, and writing, then memorizing grammatical rules such as the following will do well to improve upon your Chamorro knowledge base.

Prefixes
a-....................reciprocation marker i.e. Afa'na'gue na dos - Teach each other
acha-..............."as" "equal" or "both"
an-...................leftovers of something
cha'-................(with possessive pronouns) "don't" "shouldn't"...a warning
chat-...............negative marker, or "slightly" i.e. Chatmanhula - Lying under oath
fa'-....................to pretend, fake, or scam
fama'-...............(imperative) to make or act
fan...i an...........a place where...
ga'-....................to like or prefer/animal prefix
ge'-....................used in direction or giving directions
          i.e. Ge'haya - Go east
gi-......................at
ha (hah)-..........usually or often
iyo-..............to belong to someone or something
ka-....................to have
ke-.....................to try to do something

la'-....................a bit more, slightly

ma-....................(passive voice) used with verbs,
    i.e. **ma**+**funas** (erase)= **Mafnas** (erased).
man-..................(plural or indefinite marker)
mi-....................to have a lot of, many
mina'-...............ordinal marker, used for numbers,
    i.e. Mina'tres - Third
na'-....................to cause or make someone do something or
    one who does something/food classifier
pinat-...............too much of
san-...................directional marker (locatives)
tai-....................without, none, to not have
tak-...................comparative marker used for locations
ya-....................(superlative) used in direction and location/to be
attracted to, to enjoy

Suffixes

-an....................used in location and direction
-guan.................in spite of, something happening contrary to one's
intentions
-gui
-guiyi
-hun..................used in quoting someone
-i.......................used in referencing
-iyi
-ña....................better in comparison/his, hers, its
-ña...ki...............used in comparison
-ñaihon..............a moment, little while, a short amount of time
-on....................to be able to
-yi.....................used in referencing
-yon...................to be able to

3 FAMILY AND FRIENDS

Familia-ta
Our Family

Hi, friend. - **Hafa lai/ga'chong/che'lu.**
How are you? - **Hafa tatamanu hao?** or **Hafa mamaolek ha?**
Fine, friend. And you? - **Maolek lai yan hagu?**
I'm fine too. - **Maolek lokkue.**
How is your family? - **Hafa manatatamanu i familia-mu?**
They are not so good. - **Ti man gof maolek.**

They are fine. And your family?
Manmamaolek ha'. Yan i familia-mu?

They are fine too. - **Manmamaolek ha' lokkue.**

Come and visit us at home when you have time.
Fanmambisisita guatu gi gima yanggen guaha lugat-miyu.

Alright, if we have time.
Po'lu nai ya yanggen guaha lugat.

You too, come and visit us at our home.
Hamyo lokkue, fanmambisita.

Ok. Thank you. Bye - **Esta. Si yu'us ma'ase. Adios**
Good-bye friend - **Adios ga'chong**

Lourdes called me - **Ha agang yu' si Lourdes.**
Antonio called Lourdes - **Inagang si Lourdes as Antonio.**

This is the third time I've called you.
Este i mina'tres biahi na hu agang hao.

I will call you - **Bai hu aging hao**
I will call you back – **Bai hu aging hao tatte**

If you leave tomorrow, be sure to call mom.
An humanao hao agupa', adahi na ti un agang si Na.

Familia-ta - Our Family

nana - mother
tata - father
neni - baby
patgon - child
famagu'on - children
che'lu (lahi) - brother
che'lu (palao'an) - sister

pairasto - stepfather
mairasta - stepmother

matlina - godmother
patlinu - godfather
hadu - godson
hada - goddaughter

nanan biha/guella - grandmother
tatan bihu/guello - grandfather
ñeta - granddaughter
ñetu - grandson

bisaguello - great grandfather
bisaguella - great grandmother
besnetu - great grandson
besneta - great granddaughter
tarañeta - great great granddaughter
tarañetu - great great grandson

sotteru - young bachelor
sottera - young lady
sotteritu - teenage son
sotterita - teenage daughter
hobensitu - preteen male
hobensita - preteen female

sugra - mother-in-law
sugro - father-in-law
yetno - son-in-law
yetna - daughter-in-law
kuñada - sister-in-law
kuñadu - brother-in-law
konsugra - parents-in-law (mother)
konsugro - parents-in-law (father)

tiha - aunt
tihu - uncle
subrina - niece
subrinu - nephew
prima - cousin (female)
primu - cousin (male)

biuda - widow
biudu - widower

taotao - human being/person
palao'an - female
lahi - male

Basta i Apbladurihas!
Stop Spreading Gossip!

As you may or may not be aware, gossiping is definitely a popular Chamorro pastime as in any other culture. There are quite a few common phrases you may hear in a Chamorro gossip-fest as you would in other languages. In English, there are terms like hearing something "through the grapevine" – there's even a song and raisin commercial about it – and there's a way to say that in Chamorro as well.

Before proceeding into gossip vocabulary, it is important to explain the value of reputations in Chamorro culture. For example, when two people are talking and the first person says that they heard a bit of gossip from another person, the second person may reply in a way to discredit that source. **"Munga ma ekunguk si Marla, si tata-ña gof ya-ña mugandon salape"** (Don't listen to Marla, her father likes to gamble) is an example of this process of discreditation, saying something negative about the third person's family or reputation is often used to dispel that person's say-so. While this method may seem somewhat hilarious, it is used frequently in Chamorro conversation.

What does one's father's gambling problem have to do with anything, you may ask? Well, reputation amongst Chamorros is of importance because it is something that is not easily repaired. Therefore it's invaluable and there is a need to protect it. Yet, it may appear to be a bit unfair to judge a person based solely on the actions of their family members as the apple may sometimes fall far from the tree. Instead, one should be viewed based on their own actions and merit since we all have a tendency to judge and categorize people, whether we like to admit it or not.

So the next time you hear gossip and have the urge to intervene and be an **embilikera** or **embilikeru**, just say **Yanggin ti hagu masasangan pues taya derecho-mu para un kuentos**!

28

The following is a quick example of a Chamorro conversation involving a smidgen of gossip between two friends, Jose and Rosa:

Jose: Hey, Rosa, un tungo?
Rosa: Shh! A'gang hao mampos! Laña, tungo' mañang!
Jose: Un hunguk?
Rosa: Ekkua adai, ti hunguk.
Jose: Si Juan ha tatke i katsunes-ña gi gipot!
Rosa: Hafa?!
Jose: Tatfoi i pinalala-ña asta malagu!
Rosa: Hiningok-mu ha' enao gi telefon alaihai.
Jose: Un tungo'?!
Rosa: Ahi, Jose. Basta i apbladurihas, puta i lahi ni para usao nao umapbladot.
Jose: Hey, laña, hafa i problema-mu?
Rosa: Ti banda-mu Jose, yanggin ti hagu masasangan pues taya derecho-mu para un kuentos.

A'gang hao mampos! - You're so loud!
Ahi, ti hunguk - No, I didn't hear
Basta i apbladurihas! - Stop spreading gossip!
Basta i binaba siha - Stop the foolishness
Ekkua adai, ti hunguk - I don't know, I didn't hear
Ekkua adai, ti tungo - I don't know, I didn't know about it
Laña - an interjection like "damn!" or "shit!"
Hafa i problema-mu? - What's your problem?
Hey, un tungo? - Hey, did you know?
Hey, munga masangan! - Hey, don't say anything!

Embilikeru (m.)/**Embilikera** (f.)
Someone who interferes, a "busy-body"

You just heard that through the grapevine
Hiningok-mu ha' enao gi telefon alaihai

Don't listen to Lisa, her husband is a drunk!
Munga ma ekunguk si Lisa, sa bulacheru i asagua-ña!

Don't listen to Marla, her father likes to gamble.
Munga ma ekunguk si Marla,
si tata-ña gof ya-ña mugandon salape.

Don't listen to Juan, his mother's a whore!
Munga ma ekunguk si Juan, sa puta si nana-ña!

Don't spread "dirt" - **Munga ma machalapun**
Don't spread gossip - **Munga ma mama'famta**

There is nothing worse than a man who gossips.
Puta i lahi ni para usao nao umapbladot.

Juan pooped his pants at the party!
Si Juan ha tatke i katsunes-ña gi gipot!

He was so much in a rush, he took off!
Tatfoi i pinalala-ña asta malagu!

You are almost always the noisiest one.
Tatnai ti hagu mas burukento or Hagu mas burukento.

That's none of my business - **Ti banda-hu**
That's none of your business - **Ti banda-mu**
That's none of his/her business - **Ti banda-ña**
Learn how to whisper - **Tungo' mañang**

Don't say anything since you have no right to talk.
Yanggin ti hagu masasangan pues taya
derecho-mu para un kuentos.

Rosa put the conceited man in his place.
Si Rosa ha na'ha'yan i banidosu na taotao.

Stop your made-up story right there.
Basta i plasu-mu guenao.

You are not worth anything at all. - **Ni hafafa bali-mu.**
What in the world are you doing? - **Hafkao bidada-mu guenao?**

My brother is a back-talker - **Ekpe i che'lu-hu lahi**

I know – **Hu tungo'**
I don't know – **Ti hu tungo'**
You know – **Un tungo'**
You don't know – **Ti un tungo'**
There's no way that you can know – **Ni taimanu ti un tungo'**

Komplimento i mafañagun i patgon-mu!
Congratulations on the birth of your child!

What's his/her name?
Hayi na'an-ña?

This is Maria.
Si Maria este.

How much did he/she weigh?
Kuanto i minakka-ña?

How many inches is he/she?
Kuanto i annako-ña?

He has his father eyes.
Ha chule' i matan tata-ña.
or
Ha'osgi i matan tata-ña.

She has her mother's face.
Ha chule' i matan nana-ña.

He has his father's height.
Ha chule' i lineka tata-ña.

She has her father's smile.
Kalan si tata-ña an chumalek.

He has his mother's hair.
Ha chule' i gapotulun nana-ña.
or
Ha'osgi i gapotulun nana-ña.

She has her mother's eyebrows.
Kalan sehas nana-ña.

It is important to teach your child Chamorro.
Impottante na para un fa'ña'gue i patgon-mu ni fino' Chamorro.

Are you going to teach your child how to speak Chamorro?
Kao para un fa'ña'gue i patgon-mu ni fino' Chamorro?

You must be very proud!
Debidi un banidosa!*

He is very handsome.
Mampos bunitu.

She is very beautiful.
Mampos bunita.

Such beautiful eyes!
Bunita mampos i mata-ña!

What a beautiful smile!
Mampos bunita chumalek!

When was he/she born?
Ngai'an ni mafañagu?

What's your birthdate?
Hafa i mafañagu-mu?

Do you need anything for the baby?
Kao guaha mas un nisisita para i neni?

Do you need baby clothes or diapers?
Kao un nisisita magagu pat pañales?

Let me know if you need anything!
Natungo' yu yanggin guaha mas un nisisita!

Don't be worried, all new parents are nervous.
Cha'mu chathinasso, sa todo nuebo na man'aina man luluhan.

You'll do fine.
Siempre ha todo maolek.

You will be an excellent parent.
Mampos hao siempre maulek na saina.

Hold the baby carefully.
Hoguen maulek i neni.
or
Go'ten maulek i neni.

*Banidosa in this sense is not derogatory as it tends to mean show-off or gaudy, but in this case it means proud.

Chamorro Prepositions and Conjunctions

Prepositions

Prepositions are what links phrases, nouns and pronouns in order to form a sentence. The preposition is what introduces the object and creates a relationship within the sentence. In Chamorro, as in most any language, we have the following prepositions that are used in order to indicate logical and spatial differences in sentences:

Entre/Entalo/Gi entalo - between
Fuera di - except or outside of
Gi - in/on
Hasta - until
Kon - with
Kontra - against
Para - for
Pot - through or for
Sin - without
Tai or **Taya** - without
Yan - and

Conjunctions

Conjunctions also link words, phrases, or clauses in order to join elements of a sentence. The following words are Chamorro conjunctions used in everyday sentences:

Anai - when
Anai ha - as soon as *(for quick turn of events from bad to worse, etc)*
Antes di - before
Despues di - after
Ensigidas - as soon as
Gin - if (somewhat of a slang for Yanggin)
Kao - indicator of a question
Lao -but
Lokkue - also
Lu - nevertheless
Masea - although

Mientras - while
Na - that (past)
Nu - that (future)
Parehu - the same
Pat - or
Sa - then, due to, because
Ya - and, to connect sentences
Yan - and, to connect words
Yanggin - if

4 EDUCATION

Gi Eskuela
At School

Gi Eskuela – At School

Wake up Lani, it's time for school.
Na'fakmata si Lani sa esta oran eskuela.

The child was absent from school.
I patgon fatta gi eskuela.

I will be quiet in school.
Bai hu famatkilo gi eskuela.

I finished reading the book.
Esta munhayan hu taitai i lepblu.

I will definitely go to school tomorrow.
Siempre bai hu hanao para i eskuela agupa.

The students obeyed school regulations.
I estudiante siha ma konfotma i lain eskuela.

I was joking around with Linda at school.
Hu essitani si Linda gi eskuela.

I reminded Jose to get his book at school.
Hu na'hasso si Jose na u chule' i lepblo-ña gi eskuela.

Professor - Prufisot
Teacher (female/male) - Ma'estra/Ma'estro
Student – Estudiante
Children - Famagu'on

Book - **Lepblo**
Chair - **Siya**
Chalkboard - **Pisara**
Chalk - **Yesu**
Crayon - **Korehong**
Eraser - **Fifunas**
Kindergarten - **Kattiya**
Paper - **Pappet**

Paperclip - **Chiget pappet**
Pen - **Pluma**
Pencil – **Lapes**
Picture - **Litratu**
Rubber band - **Goma**
Ruler – **Midida**
Student's chair - **Siyan estudiante**
Student's desk - **Lamasan estudiante**
Teacher's chair - **Siyan ma'estra(o)**
Thumb tacks – **Attachuelas**
Workbook - **Kattiya pat lepblo**

What did you learn at school today?
Hafa tiningo-mu gi eskuela na ha'ane?

What did you eat today? - **Hafa unkanno na ha'ane?**
Did you behave today? - **Koti umagoguat hao na ha'ane?**
Behave - **Ketu**
What did you do? - **Hafa un cho'gue?**
Do your homework - **Cho'gue tarea-mu**

Did you finish all of your homework?
Kao un na'funhayan i tarea-mu?

If you don't finish your homework, you can't play.
Yanggin ti un cho'gue i tarea-mu,
ti un huyong hao umugandu.

Education first - **I edukasion finene'na.**
You can go outside. - **Sina hao pago humuyong.**

Facho'cho ya un cho'cho - Work and you will eat

What time do you work? - **Ki ora para un facho'cho'**
I work all the time – **Todo i tiempo macho'cho yu'.**
I work hard. – **Duru yu macho'cho.**
I'm about to begin working – **Kumeke macho'cho yu'.**

Dad, can you lend me some money, please?
Ta, na'ayao yu salappe, pot fabot?

Do you have any money? **Kao guaha salappe'-mu?**
No - **Ahe'**
That's not fair! - **Ti husto ennao!**
Come here – **Maila fan hanao guini**
Where is the store? **Manu nai gaige i tenda?**
Let's go – **Nihi ta hanao**
Can you give me a ride? **Kao siña un na ma'udai yu?**

Where do you work - **Manu nai macho'cho hao?**
I work in Garapan - **Macho'cho yu' giya Garapan.**

Hard-working – **Bunmuchachu**
Lazy – **Gagu'**

Sensia - Personality and Characteristics

Aktibu - Vivacious
Adotteru/a – Adulterer
Amama – A kiss-up, sycophant
Animosu - Brave
Ansias - Anxious
Antagonista - Antagonist
Apbladoru/a - Gossip
Atmirapble/Famao - Admirable
Attamos - Foolish
Chatilu – Stubborn, hard-headed
Chattao - Selfish
Chetnot manman – Someone "off in space"
Dakon/Embusteru – Liar
Dolle - Weakling
Dudos – Flirtatious, show-off
Embidiosu/a – Hot-headed
Embilikeru/a – Nosy, someone who interferes
Enamorao - Amorous
Fakla - One who tells tall tales
Felis/Magof - Happy
Figo' - Tenacious
Gaddai bebe' - Womanizer
Gekpo - Flighty
Goftao - Selfless
Hambiento - Avaricious
Hosguan - Full of wrath
Impetosu - Short-tempered
Ka'lak - Attractive
Konsoladot - Sympathetic
Magahet - Honest
Matapang – Stuck-up
Mathenio – Moody, snappy
Osgon – Submissive
Otguyosu – Proud
Pachang - Sissy
Salamanka – Trickster
Sentidu – Touchy, sensitive

Emotions

Aburidu/Gaddon - Confused
Ansias - Anxious
Asustao/Ma'añao - Frightened
Empachu or **O'son** - Bored
Felis/Magof - Happy
Lalalu - Angry
Loku/a – Crazy
Luhan (like the surname Lujan) - Worried
Malangu - Sick
Susto - Horrified
Timagof - Unhappy/Depressed
Tinemba ni sagu - Low energy (from being sick0
Triste - Sad

Actions and Characteristics

achetge - wink
achigo' - eyes closed
asayon - nausea
asson - lie down
atalak - glare or big bright eyes
bada - hunch-backed
bachet - blind
ba'chego'/bakchiku - slant-eyed (fyi: not a very polite term)
baila - dance
bailan lagas pat sulon - skate
chalamlam - blink
chalek - laugh
chatge - smile
chiche' - sneering teeth
dakdak i patas - tap feet
deha - squat
dengnga - bending over
dimu - kneel
eggeng - lean or bend
falagu - run

fata'chong - sit
fatigao/yafai - fatigued
foyong - slump
hila'gue - show tongue
hoflak - lick
iba' - trembling lips
kaduku - dumb/stupid
ka'dedeng - skip
kasse - tease
ke'yu - lame
kiba' - sneer
kitan - cross-eyed
lagas - glide
lekngai - stiff neck
maigo' - sleep
makaka - itchy
malangu - sick
manman - stare
matan lalalo' - angry face
muta' - vomit
muyo' - pout, frown
na'susu - to nurse
ngaha' - look up
ngangas - chew
oppop - prone position
pahya' - speech impediment
patek - kick
puti - hurt
sage' - burning sensation
sasa' - straddling
si'ok - stab
sulon - slide
tanges - cry
ta'yok - jump
ta'yok takpapa' - hop
tisu - stiff
tokcha' - pierce
toktok - hug
to'la' - to throw saliva or spit

tomba - topple
to'to' - supine position
udu - mute
uha' - gag
yayas - tired

More Expressions

Adahe - 'watch it'; A word of warning
Agun/Chamu hit/Megahit - Really?
Aike - A sarcastic 'sure'
Aike malago - You wish!
Animat - Animal
Atan baba (also **Atalaki**) - Dirty look
Banidosu/a - Show-off
Basta di babiche - Stop lying!
Basta di malaña - Stop messing around!
Basta it?! - No way?!
Brutu/a – An annoying person, moron, fool
Chagi - Try it
Che'lu - Close friend, sibling
Chenchule' - Gift/donation
Chiliguagua - Someone who is being 'the third wheel'
Dagan - Rear end, buttocks
Dekka – Poke
Deska - Flicking (especially someone's ear)
Digerro - Cheater
Dofi - Having teeth missing
Fafata - Somewhat crazy
Fama'kilo i pachot-mu - Shut your mouth
Fan hongi chadig! - Believe me!
Gi menan Yu'us - I swear to God
Kaduku/a - Stupid, crazy
Kalakas - Disgusting
Kochinu/a - Dirty
Lalalu - Angry
Lakus hit - An expression indicating disbelief
Laña - An expression used to indicate just about anything from anger to surprise

Mahaderu/a - Irritating person, imbecile

Mamahlao - Embarrassed

Mayamak - Broken

Manman - Dazed

Matapang - Stuck up (name of a Chamorro chief who had anger issues, but rightfully so)

Meme - Urine

Mutung - Stinky

Nai/Nei - A common Chamorro filler word

Nanalao - Give me a break!

Nenga Naya! - Hold on!

"Oba skoba" - The end, Fin, that's all! (A Chamorro-English blending of words; *over the broom*)

Pare/gachong - Friend

Pika - Spicy

Pikaru - Perverted, Sneaky

Poki/Debu/Chebot - Fat, Chubby

Po asu - Term for Chamorros raised in the Mainland U.S. or Chamorros who act more Western than indigenous

Pugua - Betel nut

Pupulo - Leaves eaten with betel nut

Puti tai nobiu - Single

Sape!/Anda! - A term used to shoo away animals

Take' - Feces

Tai bida - Worthless

Tai mamahlao - Shameless

Ti mamaigu si Yu'us - God never sleeps...

Toka – To get caught

Tubon Take' - Junk

Antonyms and Adjectives

Big - **Dangkolo'**
Small - **Dikike'**

Tall - **Lokka**
Short - **Ettigu**

Long - **Anaku**
Short - **Kadada**

Wide - **Feda**
Narrow - **Mafnot/Angosto**

Deep – **Tadong**
Shallow - **Natata**

High - **Hulu, Lokka**
Low - **Papa**

Fat - **Debu**
Skinny - **Soksok**

Heavy - **Makkat**
Light - **Ñalalang**

Good - **Maolek**
Bad - **Baba**

Sad - **Triste**
Happy - **Felis/Magof**

Tired - **Yayas**
Awake - **Manmata**

Scared - **Ma'añao**
Brave - **Ti ma'añao**

Strong - **Metgot**
Weak - **Ñama/Debit**

Old - **Bihu** (people)
Young - **Hoben**

Old - **Antigu/Bihu**
New - **Nuebu**

Right - **Tunas**
Wrong - **Lachi**

Friend - **Amigu/Ga'chong**
Enemy - **Enemigo**

Dry - **Anglo**
Wet - **Fotgon**

Full - **Bula**
Empty - **Basio/Taya/Hokog**

Clean - **Gasgas**
Dirty - **Applacha**

Right - **Agapa**
Left - **Akague**

Expensive - **Guaguan**
Cheap - **Baratu**

Beautiful – **Bonitu/a**
Ugly – **Chat' pago**

Hot - **Maipe**
Cold - **Manengheng**

Early - **Taftaf**
Late - **Atrasao**

Alive - **La'la'**
Dead - **Matai**

Fragrant - **Paupau**
Foul-smelling - **Mutung**

Healthy - **Homlo**
Sick - **Malangu**

Hard - **Mahetok**
Soft - **Mañaña/Mahañas**

Difficult - **Mapot**
Easy - **Ti mapot**

Sweet - **Mames**
Sour - **Ma'aksom**
Bitter - **Mala'et**

Savory - **Mannge**
Salty - **Ma'asen/Ma'asne**

Noisy - **Buruka/Kalaskas** (jingling sound)
Quiet - **Mahgong/Silensiu**

Chamorro Quotes

In learning a new language or refreshing what you know, the one thing that will help you succeed is something people just don't like: Memorization. Memorizing and repeating phrases help you to retain new words and sentences which are vital for language learning. Although tedious, repeating and memorizing vocabulary and phrases are all a part of becoming fluent in a language. Here are a few more famous quotes that you can use to help in comprehension and language retention:

Elie Wiesel

I swore never to be silent whenever and wherever human beings endure suffering and humiliation. We must take sides. Neutrality helps the oppressor, never the victim. Silence encourages the tormentor, never the tormented.

Manhula-yu na ti bai hu fama'kilo yanggin guaha na sinapit yan na mamahlao. Debi di ta lipara i dinanche na banda. I nuturalidat inayuyuda para u anuk i applacha na finatinas yan traision ni para i mamadesi. Yanggin mama'kikilo yan pomeniniti una o'obra i traidot na taotao, debi di un mumuyi i traision.

*not an exact translation, but close enough to carry the point

Edmund Burke

All that is necessary for evil to succeed
is that good men do nothing.
**Todo siha na nesesidat i finatinas Satanas,
taya i maolek na taotao siña ha chogue.**

George Santayana

Those who don't learn from history
are doomed to repeat it.
**Todo siha i ti kumunprende i historia
siempre ma ripiti ta'lo tati.**

Maya Angelou

There's nothing so pitiful as a young cynic because he has gone from knowing nothing to believing nothing.

Taya mina'ase tat komu un hoben ha taihininge sa ginen timanungo yan timanhongge.

Ralph Waldo Emerson

One must learn the language of the country he visits. Otherwise he voluntarily makes himself a great baby - so helpless and so ridiculous.

Debi di un utungo' i linguahi i tano' pat i lugat ni ha bisita. Pat u fa'ma'neni - taya ayudu yan atmariao.

Navajo Prayer

Beauty is before me, beauty is behind me. Above me and below me hovers the beautiful.

Gatbo gi mena-hu, gatbo gi tate-ku. Gi hilo-hu yan gi papa-hu mampos gatbo.

Standing Bear

Man's heart away from nature becomes hard.

Yanggin i korason taotao chago kontra i tano, i korason-ña mampos mahetok.

5 TRAVELING AND DIRECTIONS

Para manu hao?
Where are you going?

Taotao manu hao? - Where are you from?

I'm from _____.
Taotao _____ yu.

Are you African American, Hispanic, Asian American, Native American, or Pacific Islander?
Kao Afrikano Amerikanu, Ispañot, Asiano Amerikanu, Natibu Amerikanu, pat Islas Pasifiku na taotao hao?

Where did you come from? - **Ginen manu hao?**
Where are you going? - **Para manu hao?**
Are you lost? **Hafa malingu hao?**
Did you lose something? **Hafa malingu-mu?**

I'm just visiting Saipan - **Manbisisita ha yu giya Saipan**

Where do you live? **Manu nai sumasaga hao?**
I live in California – **Sumasaga yu giya California**
When were you born? **Ngai'an nai mafañagu hao?**

I was born on March 5rd, 1981
Mafañagu yu' sinku gi Matsu,
Mit nobesientos nobentaiocho (1981)

Today is my birthday! – **Pa'go mafañagu-hu!**
How old are you? – **Kuantos años hao?**
Happy Birthday - **Biba Kumpleaños**
I was born in New York – **Mafañagu yu giya New York**

How do you say that in your language?
Taimanu nai masasangan enao gi fino'-miyu?

One language is never enough
Un linguahe ni ngai'an u nahom

Para manu hao? - Where are you going?

Where is the Plumeria?
Manu gaige i Plumeria?

Is it far? - **Kao chagu?**
No, it is not far - **Ahe, ti chago**

The Plumeria is in San Roque by the ocean.
Gaige i Plumeria San Roque gi fi'on i tasi.

Are you staying at this hotel?
Sumasaga hao guini na hotel?

Yes/No - **Hunggan (or "A'a")/Ahe**
Try the Nikko - **Chagi i Nikko.**

How do I get to the Nikko?
Taimanu fatto-ku guatu gi Nikko?

Take the road towards Marpi and
just before, on your left is Nikko and
on your right will be La Fiesta Mall.
**Tunanas kattan para Makpi antes di un
fatto Makpi gi akague-mu i Nikko hotel pa'go
gi agapa-mu ti chago i Nikko i La Fiesta Mall.**

Yes, this is a good hotel.
Hunggan, gof maolek este na hotel.

Yes, this is a beautiful hotel.
Hunggan, nai gof bonito este na hotel.

Do you have any vacant rooms?
Kao guaha kuatto bakante?

Yes for only one person. - **Hunggan, lao para un taotao ha.**
How much per day? - **Kuanto gi dia?**
Eighty Dollars - **Ochenta pesos.**

How long are you going to stay?
Kuantos tiempo para sumaga-mu?

Three days only.
Para tres dias ha.

Then come on over - Pues mamaila/Pues hanao magi.

It's too far. You can't walk.
Chago dimasiao. Ti siña hao lumahu.

You have to take a car.
Nesesita un ma'uda gi kareta.

Is there a bus I can take?
Kao guaha bus siña hu chule?

No, but you can take a taxi.
Taya lao siña tinakse hao.

Excuse me - **Dispensa yu**
Excuse me, sir - **Dispensa ha, Siñot**
Thank you - **Si Yu'us ma'ase**
Good-bye - **Adios**

Is there a restaurant around here?
Manu nai guaha restoran?
or **Kao guaha restoran guini gi oriya?**

What kind of restaurant do you want?
Hafa na klasen restoran malago-mu?

Is there a Chamorro restaurant?
Kao guaha restoran Chamorro? (You can also use **"sagan chumochu"** instead of **"restoran"**)

We don't have any here.
Ti ma'usa. (lit: we don't use those)
or **Taya guini**

There is a Chamorro restaurant in Hagatña, Guam.
Guaha restoran Chamorro giya Hagatña, Guahan.

The price is reasonable and the service is good at Terry's.
Resonapble i presio yan maolek i sitbesio guihi gi as Terry's.

Can you tell me which road to follow?
Kao siña un sagani yu manu na chalan bai hu tattiyi?

If you get off from Marine Drive, take a left.
**Humuyong hao guini gi chalan Marine,
bira hao papa gi akague-mu.**

After about a mile, you'll reach Terry's.
**Kasi enao un miya na distansia
siempre matto hao gi Terry's.**

It is on the right hand/left-hand side of the road.
Gaige gi agapa-mu/akague-mu na bandan chalan.

Can you tell me where the phone is?
Kao siña un sagani yo manu guatu na gaige i telefon?

It is near the door.
Gaige guihi guatu gi fi'on i petta
or **Hihot yan i petta.**

Are you Chamorro? - **Kao Chamorro hao?**
Yes, I am Chamorro. - **Hunggan, Chamorro yu.**

Transpottasion - Transportation

Is the transportation system on the island reliable?
Kao sistema transpottasion guini gi isla siña ta angokko?

Where can I find a taxi?
Amanu ni siña para bai u sodda' i ta apapasi na taksi?

Is this the bus schedule? **Kao guiya este siha i oran i bas?**

Is it expensive to rent a car? **Kao guaguan man atkila kareta?**

Hi, can you take me to the airport?
Hafa adai, kao siña un konne' yu' para i plasan batkon aire?

Can you take me to the store?
Kao siña un konne' yu' para i tenda?

Can you take me to the hotel?
Kao siña un konne' yu' para i guma dumeskansa? (instead of
"guma dumeskansa," you can also use "hotel")

Can you take me to the nearest restaurant?
**Kao siña un konne' yu' para i mas hihot na guma
fañochuyan/sagan chumochu?**

Is it easy to get around on the island by yourself?
Kao libianu para bai ridondeha i isla ni hagu na maisa?
or **Kao libianu para bai likoku'i i isla ni guahu na maisa?**

How much do I owe you? **Kuanto hu didibi hao?**

Do you accept credit cards? **Kao un aksepta i kattan kreditu?**
Cash only! **Kas ha!**

Sorry, where is the nearest bank or ATM?
Dispensa, manu i mas hihot na banko pat i makinan salape'?

I only have $20. Is that enough?
Taya guaha-hu na bente pesos, ha. Kao nahong na ni este?

Yes, but make sure to carry extra cash on you when traveling in case of emergencies.
Hunggan, lao na siguru na un dilileng meggai na kas yangin kumarera hao sa hafa yangin matto i achaki.

I will - **Hu'u** or **Bueno**

Travel safe, and be careful!
Na safo' i karera-mu mo'na yan gof adahi!

Don't accept rides from strangers.
Cha'mu aksepta para un ma'udai i hayi na taotao.

Hitchhiking is dangerous. **Munga ma'udai kuakuet sa peligro.**

People on the island are friendly, but you must still be careful.
I taotaotano man maolek, lao debi ha un gof adahi hao.

Watch your belongings so no one steals your stuff.
Adahi i kosas-mu, ya munga di un ma sakkenguan.

Protect your valuables.
Protehi i iyo-mu ni man guaguan.

Always stay in a safe area.
Debe di un saga ni safo' na lugat.

Don't go around by yourself, take a friend.
Munga humahanao na maisa ya un liliku, konne i amigo-mu.

Sinangan Siha put Klema - Climate Phrases

It's gonna be a sunny day today - **Para somnak na ha'ani**
Partly cloudy today - **Nubladu na ha'ani**
It's gonna be a rainy day - **Para chatha'an pa'go**
It's a clear day - **Klaru na ha'ani**
A cloudy day. It's to be -implied statement - **Motmo na ha'ani**

I predicted the weather for tomorrow.
Ha adibina i tiempo para agupa.

A heavy rain cloud is coming - **Mamamaila' i hemhom uchan**
It rained today - **Uchan pa'go**
It's raining! - **Ai sa' u'uchan!**
It's raining in San Vicente - **U'uchan gi San Vicente**
It's going to be sunny today - **Para somnak pa'go**
Sprinkling only - **Tette ha'**
What a windy day - **Guaifon na ha'ani**
Blow out the candle - **Guaife i danges**
Plenty of (typhoon) wind - **Bula manglo' yanggen pakyo**
Air out the room - **Na'inaire i kuatto**

We have adapted to California's weather.
In adapta ham gi kleman California.

Gi Tenda - At the Store

Do you carry women's clothes?
Kao un kakatga magagun famalao'an? or
Kao un bebende magagun famalao'an?

Do you carry men's clothes?
Kao un kakatga magagun lalahe?

Do you carry children's clothes?
Kao un kakatga magagun famagu'on?

Do you carry Michael Kors?
Kao un kakatga Michael Kors?

This is in style. **Este pago' i modelu.**
That's so expensive! **Mampos guaguan enao!**
Do you have any discounts? **Kao guaha deskuenta?**

Do you have this in a size 5?
Kao guaha mina'sinku na mineddong?

This is too big. Do you have a size smaller?
Mampos dangkolo este. Kao guaha mas dikike na mineddong?

This is too small. Do you have a bigger size?
Mampos dikike esta. Kao guaha mas dangkolo na mineddong?

This is a perfect fit. I'll take it.
Esta pago i prifekto. Bai hu chule este.

I like this color, but I don't like that other color.
Ya-hu este na kulot, lao ti ya-hu i otro na kulot.

Does this make me look fat?
Kao haña yommok i ma atan-hu este?

No! You look great in that dress!
Ahe! Bonitu ma atan-mu nu enao na bestidu!
(or chinina instead of bestidu)

You seem like you lost some weight.
Kalan masoksok hao pago.

Oh, you're just saying that to be nice.
Ai, un sasangan ha enao pot para un na magof ha yu.

I'd like to buy a souvenir t-shirt from Saipan.
Malago yu para bai fahan rikuetdo na magagu ni ginen Saipan.

Do you carry any Chamorro souvenirs here?
Kao un kakatga hafa na fina rikuetdon Chamorro guini?

Isla - Island

Air - Aire
Blow (wind) - Guaifi
Breeze, wind - Manglo
Coconut tree - Tronkon niyok
Coconut - Niyok
Fish - Guihan
Moon - Pulan
Ocean - Tasi
Rain - Uchan
Rain (sprinkling) - Tette
River - Saddok
Sand - Unai
Shell - Tahgong
Shore - Kanton tasi
Sun - Atdao
Sunshine/Sunny - Somnak
Turtle - Haggan
Typhoon - Pakyo
Waterfall - Tingteng/Pineddong Hanom
Windy - Guaifon

Directions (Guam)
North – **Lagu, San lagu*** (toward north)
South – **Haya, San haya**
East – **Katan, San katan**
West – **Luchen, San luchen**

Directions (Saipan)
North – **Kattan, San kattan**
South – **Luchan, San luchan**
East – **Haya, San haya**
West – **Lagu, San lagu*** (toward north)

*San lagu is also a term used to refer to the United States

Marianas Anthem

Gi talo gi halom tasi
Nai gaige tano-hu
Ayo nai siempre hu saga
Malago' hu
Ya un dia bai hu hanao
Bai fatto ha' ta'lo
Ti siña hao hu dingo
O tano-hu

CHORUS:
Mit beses yan mas
Hu saluda hao
Gatbo na islas Marianas
Hu tuna hao

In the middle of the sea
Is where my home is
That is where I will spend my days
It is my desire
If I ever leave this place
One day I will return
For I can never leave you
O land of mine

CHORUS:
A thousand times and more
I will honor and salute you
Beautiful islands of the Marianas
Glory be to you

Guam Hymn

Fañohge Chamorro
Put i tano´-ta
Kanta i ma tuna-ña
Gi todu i lugat
Para i onra
Para i gloria
Abiba i isla
Sen parat.
Todu i tiempo
I pas para hita
Yan ginen i langet
Na bendision
Kontra i piligru
Na´fansafo´ ham,
Yu´us prutehi
I islan Guam.

Stand ye, Chamorros
For your country,
And sing her praise
From shore to shore,
For her honor
For her glory,
Exalt our island
Forever more.
May everlasting
Peace reign o´er us
May heaven's blessing
Come to us
Against all perils
Do not forsake us
God protect
Our island, Guam.

Foreign Loan-Words in Chamorro

The Chamorro language over the course of hundreds of years of colonization and trade have led to a significant level of foreign influence on the indigenous language. This, in turn, has created a mixture of Spanish, German, Japanese, and English that have shaped the everyday vocabulary of Chamorro speakers. Below, you'll find the different origins of commonly used foreign words in Chamorro. Spanish, however, remains the most dominant of the outside influences.

Spanish Influence

Since the Spanish arrived in 1521, their language has proven to be the most influential to the Chamorro language, which created a nearly irreversible amount of loss to original Chamorro words. Their influence wasn't exactly welcomed to put it lightly, but the outcome was detrimental to the language nonetheless. Below are just a few examples of Spanish words that are either used in Chamorro or Chamorrocized Spanish terms used in everyday speech.

Examples:

ESPIA/ESPIA
Spanish - to spy
Chamorro - to look for

Spanish/Chamorro word
LIBRO/LEPBLO - book
VERDE/BETDE - green
ESPEJO/ESPEHU - mirror
CUENTOS/KUENTOS - talk
CUANTO/KUANTO - how much?
PUERTA/POTTA - door
COBARDE/KOBATDE - coward
QUE HORA ES/KI ORA GENAO - what time is it?

English Influence

The English influence in the Marianas is most distinct on Guam. Guam tends to use loan words from English nowadays as Saipan tends to gravitate towards borrowing Japanese words.

Japanese Influence

Although the CNMI tends to borrow Japanese words, there are a few words most Chamorros on Guam or the CNMI will be able to recognize and use:

soba - soup (This Japanese word is actually borrowed from Portuguese)
zori - slippers (may sound like jori, depending where the speaker is from)

However, the CNMI does use Japanese words that some Guamanian Chamorros don't regularly use:

chirigami - toilet paper
denki - flashlight

German Influence

The word morgen was mentioned in tan essay by Peter Aldan, as a greeting in Saipan, which can be traced to the German administration in the early 1900s. The word is derived from the German "Guten Morgen" or good morning. While there isn't a tremendous German influence in Chamorro, there are a few German surnames of Chamorro families. For example:

Anderson
Bauer
Baumeister
Boyer
Hoffschneider

6 MEDICAL AND EMERGENCY SITUATIONS

Bukabulariun Mediku
Medical Terminology

Bukabulariun Mediku - Medical Terminology

How do you feel? - **Hafa sinintete-mu?**
I will get help - **Bai hu hanao ya bi fan aligao ayudu**
He/She is bleeding - **Mahahaga**
He/She is breathing - **Humahahgong**
He/She is not breathing - **Ti humahahgong**

I performed CPR, but there is still no response.
Hu na'i CPR, lao ti humahahgong or
Hu chogue na'i cpr, lao ti humahagong ha.

I feel fine - **Maolek sinintete-ku**
I feel bad - **Baba sinintete-ku**
I feel cold - **Mahengheng sinintete-ku**
I feel tired - **Yayas sinintete-ku**
I feel hungry - **Ñalang sinintete-ku**
I feel faint - **Kalan para bai hu lalangu**
I feel dizzy - **Bulachu sinintete-ku** or **Bulachu ilu-hu**
I don´t feel up to it - **Taya ganas-hu**
Right now I don´t feel like it – **Pa'go taya ganas-hu**
I have no feeling in my legs - **Taya sinintete-ku gi patas-hu**
I am in pain - **Puti yu** or **Mamadedesi yu**
I hurt my ankle - **Una puti i bayogu patas-hu**
Don't move - **Munga kumalantin**
Stay right here - **Ketu guenao**
Wait here - **Nangga guini**
My elbow hurts - **Puti i kudu-hu**

I am a doctor/nurse/paramedic.
Doktot/Enfetmera/Mediku yu.

Where does it hurt? - **Manu i puti-mu?**
Does this hurt? - **Kao puti este?**

On a scale of 1-10, ten being highest, how much does it hurt?
Yanggin unu asta i mina'dies, dies i mas tatkilo, taimanu puti-ña?

Are you bleeding? - **Kao mahahaga hao?**
Can you see me? - **Kao siña un li'e' yu?**
Can you hear me? - **Kao siña un hunguk yu?**

Do you know where you are?
Kao un tungu manu na gaige hao?

How many fingers am I holding up?
Kuanto na kalulot i u hahatsa?

What's today's date? - **Hafa na ha'ane pa'go?**
You're going to be okay - **Siempre maolek hao ha' todo**
I'm going to keep checking on you - **Bai hu sigi ha chumek hao**

We're going to keep you here a little while longer
Bai un sustene ñaihon hao guini.

This is a vaccine - **Dulok este**
This is a painkiller - **Amot para umagong i puti-mu este**
We must run more tests - **Debi di tasigi ha chumek hao**
You will need bed rest - **U nisisita umason**
You need an I.V. - **U nisisita dulok sustansia**
I'm going to give you an injection - **Bai hu dulok hao pa'go**
This will hurt for only a moment - **Un rattutu ha i puti-ña**

Do you have diabetes in your family?
Kao man daibitis i familia-mu?

You need to lose weight.
Un nisista para un ribaha i libras-mu.

Do you not exercise at all?
Kao taya kinalamten mu?

Watch what you eat, and exercise.
Atan hafa un kanno, yan na kalamten i brinabu-mu.

Be active at least thirty minutes a day most days of the week.
Kalamten masea trenta minutus gi ha'ane, kuantos dias gi semana.

There are some people with diabetes, but do not notice any signs.
Guaha taotao man daibitis, lao taya na maripara i siñat.

Change into the hospital gown.
Tulaika ya un usa i magagon espitat.

You can change back into your regular clothes
Siña pago minagago hao ni magago-mu.

Follow directions - **Tattiyi i direksion**
Open your mouth - **Baba i pachot-mu**
Stick out your tongue - **Laknos i hila'mu**
Say "Ah" - **Sangan "ah"**
Turn your head and cough - **Bira i ilu mu yan lo'lo**
Look forward - **Atan mo'na**
Touch your toes - **Pacha i kalulot patas-mu**

Get well soon!
Puedi homlo hao ti apmam!
or
Chaddek una homlo hao!

Tataotao - Body

abdomen - tuyan
ankle - bayogu
anus - madulok dagan
arch - atkos
arm - brasu
armpit - fa'fa'
artery - gugat korason
back - tatalo'
bald - boyu' or dakngas
belly - estomagu
belly button - apuya'
biceps - cha'ka
bladder - bihiga
blood - haga'
bone - to'lang
brain - titanos
buttocks - dagan
calf - sensin patas
cartilage - gekmon
cheeks - fasu
chest, bosom - ha'of
chin - achai
collarbone - to'lan apaga
crotch - afa'fa
eardrum - bahiga
ear - talanga
elbow - tommon kannai
eyebrow - sehas
eyelash - babali mata
eyelid - lassas babali
eyes - atadok
face - mata
finger - kalulot
fingernail - papakes
fingertip - puntan kalulot
fist - trompon
follicle - folikolo'

foot - addeng
forearm - kannai
forehead - ha'i
gums - fokson
hair - gapotulu
hand - kannai
head - ulu
heart - korason
heel - dedeggo
hip - ñanggo or tatayo'
index finger - tatancho
inner thigh - petnas
intestines - tilipas
joint - kuyontura
kidney - riñon
knee - tommo
kneecap - bayogu
knuckle - bayogu
leg - addeng
ligament - gugat
lips - labios
little finger - kalanke
lungs - gofes
lymph glands – tumates agagamu (also tonsils)
marrow - balaso'
middle finger - kalulot talo'
mole - do'an
moustache - bigoti
mouth - pachot
muscle - gugat
neck - aga'ga'
nerve - netbio
nipple - akado'
nose - gui'eng
palm - patma
penis - chile'
pores - maddok tataotao
posture - attura
prostate - prostata

rectum - galabok
rib – bariya/kostiyas (ribs/ribcage)
ring finger - kalulot anulat
scalp - lassas ulu
scrotum - dodole
shin - kaniya
shinbone - to'lang satnot
shoulder - apaga
shoulder blade - palitiya
side - kalaguak
sideburns - patiyas
sinus - seno'
skin - lassas
spine - espinasu
stomach - estomagu
teeth - nifen
temple - sentidu
testicle - bolabola
thigh - cha'chaga
throat - guetgueru
thumb - da'ma'gas
toe - da'ma'gas
toenail - papakes
tongue - hula' or lenggua
tonsils - tumates aga'ga
tooth – nifen
torso - torso
vagina - bebe
vein - gugat
waist - sintura
wart - du'an or nanaso'
wrist - muñekan kannai

I Minalangu Siha - Medical Conditions

ache, pain - puti
allergic - cha'otña or chuma'ot
allergies - sinago
amputee - manka
arthritis - putin to'lan
asthma - guha
asthma attack - ataken guha
bite - inakka
bleeding - mahagga'
blood blister - luga' haga'
blood sugar - mames haga'
bloody - kahaga'
blurred vision - osgon
broken bone - mahlok
bruise - dinigridu or malassas
cancer - kanset
chest cold - mafñot a'of
concussion - pangpang
conscious - mamaolek
constipation - pinidos
cough - lo'lo'
cut (in skin) - chinachak
dead, death – matai, finaitai
dental filling - empaste
diabetes - daibitis
diabetic - diabetiku
diarrhea - nina'ye masisinik
disease - chetnot, yafyaf (skin)
dislocated - akaleng, apling
drown - matmos
earache - putin talanga
ear infection - mañugo' talanga
earwax - kulakong talanga
faint - lalangu
fever - kalentura
hallucination - manguiguifi
hayfever - kalentura

head cold - sinago
headache - malinek ulu
heart-attack - ataken korason
heartburn - putin stomagu
hemorrhoids - pudos
high blood-pressure - tatkilo' haga
hyperglycemic - tatkilo' mames haga'
hypoglycemic - tapapa mames haga'
illness - minalangu
infection - mañetnot
injury - che'tan or dañu
malaria - kalentura ginen i ñohmon na tano
malignant - tairemediu
maltreatment - mattratu
menstruate - rekla, rumekla
menstruation - rekla, mahaga'
motion sickness - bulachun aire (land) bulachun tasi (sea)
nausea – chatguiya; tumaiganas (no appetite)
nosebleed - mahagga' gui'eng
obese - lodo
paralysis - litiku
poison - binenu
pulse, heartbeat - potso
rabies - rabia
rash - bosbos, satpuyidos
respiration - humagong
scarlet fever - eskatlatina
snakebite - na'ka kulepbla
snoring - lannan
sore (adj) - mahalang
sore (n) - hirida
stomach ache - putin stomagu
throbbing pain - mandedeska
toothache - putin nifen
tuberculosis - tibi
tumor - mandoko' na chetnot
unconscious - timamaolek
venom - binenu
vomit - muta'

Isao - Crime

Accomplice - Komplisi
Accuse – Akusa
Accuse falsely - Faiseknani
Accuser – Akusadot
Arrest – Aresta, Arestao (past tense)
Car theft – Sakin kareta
Crime – Isao (same word for 'sin')
Criminal – Kriminat
Criminal Justice – Hustisia Kriminat
Detain – Po'lonñaihon/Madeteneñaihon
Drunkenness - Binilachu
Guilty – Lachi, Punu'on
Felony - Felunia
Injustice – Inechong, Inhuestisia
Innocent – Inosente, Tai'isao
Interrogate – Abirigua, Eksamina
Interrogator – Abiriguadot
Intoxicated – Bulachu
Investigate – Imbestiga, Guaddok (Slang)
Investigation – Imbestigasion
Jail (n) – Tribunat/Presu
Jail (v) - Pongle
Judge - Hues
Justice - Hustisia
To be under investigation - Enkaosa
Law – Lai
Lawyer - Abugadu
Money laundering - Sakililok
Murder – Mamuno
Murderer - Pipino
Murderous - Pekno
Mystery – Titungon na minagahet
Perjury - Chatmanhula
Protest - Protesta
Punish - Kastiga
Punishment - Kastigu
Rape – Biulasion

Suspect – Suspecha
Suspicion – Suspecho
Suspicious – Suspechao
Testify – Testiguye
Testimony - Testimonio
Theft – Saki
Thief – Saki
Under oath – Manhula
Witness - Testigu

Don't lie, cheat, or steal
Munga mandagi, munga dumegeru, munga mañaki

Leave me alone!
Sappe!/Litira hao!/Basta ma estotba yu!

Help! Fire! Stop!
Ayuda! Guafe! Basta!

Call the police!
Agang i polisia!

I Beteranu Siha - Military Veterans

I don't want to lose this war, and neither do you.
Ti malagu yu mapedde nu este na gerra, tampoku hao.

Those who haven't been to war, have no idea how horrible it is.
Todo siha ayu i ti mangerra, taya tiningo-ñiha hafa taimanu i mina'añao yan pinadesi.

Don't listen to everything the media tells you.
Munga ma ekunguk todo siha i masasangan na asunto.

Support the troops.
Supotta i sindalun-ta siha.

God bless our troops.
Yu'us bendisi i sindalun mami siha.

Half of my heart is in Iraq.
Lameta i korason-hu esta gaige giya Iraq.

My son is in Iraq.
I lahi-hu gaige giya Iraq.

My daughter is in Afghanistan.
I haga-hu gaige giya Afghanistan.

Many died during the war.
Duranten i gera bula manmatai.

The VA should be helping veterans.
I VA debi di u ayuda i beteranu siha.

People sleep peaceably in their beds at night only because soldiers stand ready to do violence on their behalf.
Todo i taotao mantrankilo manmaigu gi puengge sa mangaige i sindalu siha malisto para u ma protehi hafa na achaki.

If you haven't been in combat,
do us all a favor and keep your mouth shut.
Yanggin taya hao ni gumerra,
fa'tinas i fabot yan huchom i pachot-mu.

Have respect for the dead.
Debi di u guaha respeto para i manmatai siha.

Our future is not only dependent on what the government does, but
also community involvement in how we shape our future.
Futtura-ta ahe' ti ha depende gue' ha' gi aksion i gubietno, lao
sumasaonao lokkue i komunidat gi maditetmina i futtura-ta.

Tomorrow, our children will judge the action we take today.
Agupa, i famagu'on-ta u ha husga i aksion-ta nipara ta chogue
pa'go.

Adverbs

guini - here
este magi - here!
guenao/enao nai/guenao nai - there
guenao guato/enao guato nai - there!
guihi/ayo nai - there (away from speaker)
ayo guato/guihi guato - over there (far)

Adverbs for location

san hilo/san hulo - above
san papa - below, beneath
san mena/san mona - in front, before
san tati - behind
san halom - inside
san hiyong/san huyong - outside
gi magin - on this side
guenao na banda – on that side
gi otro banda - on the other side
gi agapa - on the right
gi akague - on the left
manu/mange - where
ginen manu enao – from where
para manu - where to
masea manu - anywhere
ni manu - nowhere
gi todo na lugat/todo ha nai - everywhere

Adverbs for time

pa'go na ha'ane - today
nigap - yesterday
gi painge - last night
di ma'pos na ha'ane - the day before yesterday
agupa - tomorrow
nagupaña - the day after tomorrow

pa'go ha - immediately
pa'go – now
hagas – happened before
siempre ha/chaddek - sooner
naya – break time/getting air/cooling off
laftaftaf/chaddek - eariler
seso - often
halak - seldom
guaha nai - a few times
taya nai - never
siempre - always
kada rato - every minute
kada diha -daily
esta - already
trabia - not yet
ta'lo - again, once more
atrasao - too late
esta despues – until later
hasta lamona - until later tonight
ñgai'an - when?

antes - before
despues - after

gi chatanmak - dawn, very early in the morning
taftaf - early in the morning
gi eggan - in the morning
gi taloani - at noon
gi ha'ane - daytime
gi pu puenge - in the evening
gi puenge - at night
gi tatalopuenge - at midnight
lamona - tonight

desde i abmam - since the old days

Adverbs for comparison

hafa taimano - how?
pareho - equal, same
taiguini – as/like this
kalan - like, such as
mas - more
menos - less
hungan/hu'u - yes, yeah
ahe'/sen ahe' - no, absolutely not
buente - maybe, possibly
ada? - is it possible?
ti siña - impossible

mandagi - false, wrong
magahit – certain/true

megai - much
dididi - little
demasiao - too much

7 FIESTAS AND DINING OUT

Nengkanno yan Gimen
Food and Drinks

Fiesta! – Party!

Let's go to the party! **Nihi para i gupot!**

Why are there so many fiestas in the Marianas?
Hafa na mampos gupot giya Marianas?

Explain it to me. **Esplika enao.**

Each village honors their patron Catholic saint with a fiesta.
Kada songsong ma onra i patron Katoliko Santos ya mana guaha fiesta.

Everyone cooks and shares their food with guests – even if they're strangers.
Kada kusineru pat kusinera mapatte i nengkanno para i bisita maseha estrangheru (or **pat para hayi na taotao**).

We go from house to house and eat.
Man hanao hit kada guma para ta fan boka.

Food tents and tables are usually set up outside the person's home.
Kada guma guaha tento yan lamasa ya ma planta i nengkanno gi sanhiyong para i taotao.

People in the village cook all day and night to prepare.
Kada songsong i taotao man nalagu ha'aneyan puengi ni para umapripara.

People from all over are invited to join in eating.
Todo i taotao man ma kombida para u fan saonao manboka.

There is Chamorro music, good food, and nice people.
Guaha dandan Chamorro, guaha mangge na nengkanno, yan man gatbo na taotao (or **i taotao man atendidu**)

I like this tradition. **Hu guaiya este na kustumbre.**

It's nice that all these families get together and share their food with strangers.
Bonitu este sa todo i familia man dana ya mapatte i nengkanno para i estrangheru.

It's a fun tradition. **Na magof este na kustumbre.**

It's important that every Chamorro knows how to cook Chamorro food.
Impottante na kada Chamorro debe di u ke'tungo taimanu ma nalagu nengkanno Chamorro.

There are recipe books, but it's best to learn from an elder who knows the traditions. **Guaha lepblo ni para un tungo' munalagu, la maolek-ña yangin umeyak hao gi manamko** (or **i manaina niha tungo' i kustumbre**)

Can I have your recipe?
Siña un na iyo ni resipe/ i lepblon mannungo' munalagu.

No, it's a family secret! Just kidding with you.
Ti siña sa sekreton i familia este! Hu essitani hao ha.

Gi Sagan Chumocho' – At the Restaurant

What would you like to order? **Hafa malago-mu para un otden?**
Do you have anything without fish? **Kao guaha otro ki guihan?**
This is a seafood restaurant. We have rice.
Este na guma i fañochuyan puru ha guihan. Guaha hineksa.

I need something gluten-free. **Hu nisisita masea na gluten-free.**

I'm allergic to shellfish.
Cha'ot-hu i do'gas guihan or **Karakot na guihan siha.**

You should not be eating in a seafood restaurant if you have bad allergies.
Ti debi un chocho gi guma fanñochuyan ni puru ha na tasi yanggin guaha cha'otmu.

It's dangerous. Do you have any other food allergies?
Peligro enao. Kao guaha mas cha'otmu nengkanno'?

There is a BBQ restaurant down the road.
Guenao papa na chalan guaha (BBQ) i tiniño na sagan chumocho'.

Do you have anything other than pork?
Kao guaha maseha hafa ki katnen babui?

Do you have vegetarian options?
Kao guaha gollai ni siña bai hu ayek?

What do you have for the special today?
Gi espesiat na ha'ane, hafa guaha-mu?

What are the soups of the day?
Hafa na klasen kaddu pa'go na ha'ane?

What kind of beverages do you have?
Hafa na klasen gimen guaha-mu?

Do you have mixed drinks or any other alcohol besides beer?
Kao guaha matempla na gimen, pat otro na klasen maneska fuera di setbesa?

I'm Vegan, and I'd like more options.
Guahu Vegan yu, yan malago-hu mampos kadda.

Can I get the check please? **Siña un na iyu ni chek fan?**

We're going to go. **Bien fan hanao.**
Here you are. **Estagui hao.**

The food was great.
Mampos maolek i krisidu or Mangge i nengkanno'.

The food was terrible.
Teripble i nengkanno'.

The food was so-so/okay.
Maolek ha i nengkanno' para i tiempo.

I'll definitely come back to this restaurant.
Bai hu na siguru na bai hu fatto ta'lo tatte guini na sagan chumo'cho'.

I'll never come back to this restaurant.
Ni ngai'an nai bai hu fatto magi guini na sagan chumo'cho'.

It's my daughter's birthday, can you sing happy birthday and bring out dessert?
Kao siña un kantayi i haga'hu sa pa'go na ha'ane i kumpleaños-ña yan lokkue chule magi i fina'mames?

Ma'ho-yu
I'm thirsty

Kao malago hao gumimen?
Would you like to drink something?

Ahe', nahong yu esta setbesa.
No, I've had enough beer already.

A'a, malago yu' Coke.
Yes, I want a Coke.

I'm hungry - **Ñalang-yu**

Kao malago hao chumocho?
Would you like to eat something?

A'a, malago yu' chumocho.
Yes, I want to eat.

Nope, that's okay.
Munga yu'.

I like fish. - **Ya-hu guihan.**
I don't like fish. - **Ti ya-hu guihan.**

How much is this?
Kuanto baliña este?

Gollai - Vegetables

abuchuelas - green beans
addo' (gollai tasi) - seaweed
ahos - garlic
alageta - avocado
atmagosu - bittermelon
birenghenas - eggplant
chuchumeka - lima beans
donne' pika - chili pepper
fafalu - banana bud
fakka' - inner stem of taro
friholes - long beans
hagon donne' - hot pepper leaf
hagon suni - taro leaf
ilotes - corn on the cob
kaddagan - a vegetable that tastes like broccoli
kalabasa - long squash kalamasa - pumpkin
kankun - swamp cabbage spinach
kiukamba pat pipinon ensalada - cucumber
ma'is - corn
monggos - mongo beans
nappa' - Chinese cabbage
puntan chuchumeka - lima tips
puntan kalamasa - pumpkin tips
puntan kamuti - sweet potato tips
rades - raddish
ripoyu - cabbage
siboyas - onions
sigidiyas - wing beans
tumates - tomatoes
yetbabuena - mint

Frutas - Fruit

aga' - banana
alageta - avocado
anonas - custard apple
ates - sweetsop or sugar apple

bilembines - star apple
chandia - watermelon
granada - pomegranate
ibba' - sour grapes
laguana - soursop
lalanghita - tangerine
kahet - orange
kahet ma'gas - grapefruit
kakaguates - peanuts
kamachili - kamachili
kikamas - sweet turnip
lalangha - big lemon
lemon adamelong - red, yellow, or green lemon
lemon china - lemon (smoother skin lemon, very sour)
lemon riat - lemon (kalamanchi) riat is literally dime
makupa - mountain apple
mangga - mango
manha - young coconut
mansana - apple
mansanita - mansanita
melon - melon
niyok - coconut
piña - pineapple
pi'ot - sweet sour wild berry/green olives
      (grows near rocky areas and salt water)
pipinu - cucumber
talisai - Indian almond
tupu - sugar cane

Chamorro Dishes

Atolin Mais - Corn chowder
Chalakilis - Chicken and corn
Chorizos Españot - Spanish sausage
Chorizos Pakpak - Chamorro sausage
Empañadas – Meat-filled turnover
Estufao - Stew
Finadene' - Spicy Chamorro sauce

Fritada – Blood stew with various animal organs
Hineksa aflitun Spam – Spam fried rice
Hineksa agaga' – Red rice
Kadu - Soup
Kadun Pika - Spicy chicken dish
Kari - Curry
Kelaguen Binadu - Marinated venison in vinegar & hot peppers
Kelaguen Manuk– Chicken with lemon, ginger, and other spices
Neksa Balensiana - Spanish rice
Pado'lalo - Spicy fried eggplant
Saibok – Cook with coconut
Tamales gisu - Chamorro tamales
Titiyas - Tortillas

Mirinda - Afternoon Snack

Biskuchu – Crackers
Guma' fañochuyan – Snack bar
Inafliton batatas – Potato chips
Inafliton lemmai – Breadfruit chips
Kesu – Cheese
Mirinda – Afternoon snack
Batatas – Potatoes
Biskuchu - Crackers
Chotda – Plantain
Dagu - Yam
Dokdok – Seeded breadfruit
Fadang – Federico palm
Friholes - Beans
Hineksa – Cooked rice
Hutu – Seed from breadfruit
Ilotes – Corn on the cob
Kamuti – Sweet potatoes
Krakas - Crackers
Lemmai – Breadfruit
Ma'is - Corn
Mendioka – Tapioca
Pan - Bread

Pugas – Uncooked rice
Suni – Taro
Titiyas - Tortillas

Condiments

Fina'denne' – Chamorro hot sauce
Mantekiya – Butter
Mantekiyan kakaguates – Peanut butter
Miet – Honey
Mostasa - Mustard
Yam – Jam, jelly

Gimen - Drinks

Agi – Fermented fruit liquor
Aguayente - Liquor
Binu – Wine
Cha - Tea
Chigo' fruta – Fruit juice
Chigo' gollai – Vegetable juice
Chigo' manha – Young coconut juice
Chigo' niyok – Coconut juice
Hanom - Water
Inestila – Liquor made from banana, etc.
Kafe – Coffee
Leche - Milk
Limunada – Lemonade
Punche – Mixed drink
Setbesa – Beer
Soda - Soda
Tuba – Fermented juice from bud of coconut tree

Fina'mames - Dessert

Ahu – Grated coconut in sugar water
Apigige' – Grilled young coconut
Brohas – Sponge cake
Buchibuchi – Fried turnover
Buñelos aga – Banana doughnut
Buñelos dagu – Yam doughnut
Buñelos manglo' – Bread doughnut
Champuladu – Chocolate rice
Chukulati - Chocolate
Flan – Caramel custard
Guyuria – Firm cookies/jawbreakers
Kalamai – Corn pudding
Kanden niyok – Coconut candy
Kek Chamorro – Chamorro cake
Konsetban papaya – Candied papaya
Latiya – Pudding and angel food cake
Madoya – Fried banana
Pastet - Turnover
Rosketti – Shortbread

Katne & Guihan – Meat & Fish

asuli - eel
ayuyu - coconut crab
chachalon - pork rind
chada - eggs
do'gas - sea shell
fanihi - fruit bat
fritadan babui - pork chitterling
fritadan guaka - beef chitterling
fritadan mannok - chicken chitterling
guihan - fish
haggan - turtle meat
hammon - ham
kunehu - rabbit
mahongang - lobster
mannok - chicken

katnen babui - pork
katnen binadu - deer meat
katnen chiba - goat meat
katnen guaka - beef
katnen karabao - carabao meat
katnen notte - whole corned beef
pabu - turkey
paluma - bird
panglao - crab
pahgang - clam
tapon - baby clam
uhang - shrimp

Pronouns

There are two types of regular pronouns in the Chamorro language that are demonstrated as follows in the 1st person and plural forms:

hita – we as in 'you and I' (inclusive)
hame – we as in 'they and I' or 'he and she,' discounting the 2nd person (exclusive)

Personal Pronouns

There are two types of personal pronouns in the Chamorro language which consist of either long or short versions:

Long Form****Short Form***English Equivalent
Guahu…..............yu…....................I
Hagu…................hao…..................you
Guiya…..............gue…..................he/she
Hita…..................hit…...................we (inclusive)
Hame…...............ham…................we (exclusive)
Hamyo…............hamyo…............you (plural)
Siha…..................siha…..................they

Possessive Pronouns

Personal pronouns in the Chamorro language are used in a suffix form and are divided into the three following groups:

People

hu/ku….........my
mu…............your
ña…..............his/hers/its
ta…...............our (inclusive)
mame….........our (exclusive)
miyu…..........your (plural)
ñiha…...........their

Animals

gahu…..........my
gamu…..........your
gaña…............his/hers/its
gata…..............our (inclusive)
gamame….......our (exclusive)
gamiyu…........your (plural)
gañiha…..........their

Inanimate Objects

iyoku…............my
iyomu…...........your
iyoña…..............his/hers/its
iyota…..............our (inclusive)
iyonmame…......our (exclusive)
iyonmiyu….......your (plural)
iyonñiha…........their

8 DATING AND ROMANCE

Hu Guaiya Hao
I Love You

Gi Kachido – At the Movies

Let's go see a movie!
Nihi ta hanao ya ta keli'i i kachido!
("**mubi**" can also be used instead of "**kachido**")

What kind of movie do you want to watch?
Hafa malago-mu na kachido para ta li'i?

I love romantic movies. **Ya-hu i man guaiyayon na kachido.**
I like scary movies. **Ya-hu i man na ma'añao na kachido.**
("**bubulao**" can also be used instead of **ma'añao**)

Well, I don't like scary movies.
Ombre, ti ya-hu i bubulao na kachido.

Do you like action films? **Kao ya-mu aksion na kachido?**

Sometimes, but too much fighting can become boring to me.
Guaha na biahe, lao mampos na mumu ya hana o'son yu.

Well, romantic movies are kind of the same too.
Bueno, i man guaiyayon na kachido kalan parehu ha lokkue.

I know, but can we go watch that new comedy movie.
Hu tungo' ha, lao siña ta hanao ya ta li'e i nuebu na komeya?
("**na'chalek na kachido**" can also be used for "comedy film")

I hear it's such a good movie!
Hu hungok na mampos maolek na kachido.

I hear it's a terrible movie. **Hu hungok na baba na kachido.**
("**teripble**" can also be used instead of "**baba**" to describe something
as bad or terrible)

Okay, let's just rent a movie at home and eat popcorn in our pajamas.
**Hu'u, nihi ya ta atkila i kachido para guato gi gima yan ta
cho'cho' popcorn ya ta chininan maigo.**

Sounds like a good idea. **Kalan maolek na hinasso.**

How much are movie tickets? **Kuanto baliña i tiket i kachido.**

Which film is better? Godfather I or Godfather II?
Hafa na kachido mas maolek? I Patlinu uno pat I Patlinu dos?

I like both, but Godfather III was terrible!
Todo i dos ya-hu, lao I Patlinu tres i mas baba!

Movies are expensive these days.
Mampos guaguan i kachido na tiempo.

Let's wait until a movie comes out that we both like, then we'll go.
Po'lo ya esta ki u huyong esta na kachido ni ya-ta, despues ni ta hanao.

Hu Guaiya Hao! – I Love You!

Below a few phrases and vocabulary words in Chamorro that are appropriate for Valentine's Day or any day, depending on how much of a romantic you are.

Kiridu (male) Kirida (female) - Sweetheart
Nobiu - Boyfriend
Nobia - Girlfriend
Asagua-hu - My Spouse

Guiaya - Love
Hu guaiya hao - I love you
Mampos hao guaiyayon - You're so lovey-dovey
Gofli'e - Love (platonic)
Guiaya - Love (romantic)
Aguaiya - Love affair
Amantes - Lovers
Amante - Lovely, lovable

Regalu -Gift
Flores - Flowers
Kahitan chukulati - Box of chocolates
Mames - Candy
Kattan guinaiya - Love letter
Kantan guinaiya - Love song
Sinente - Feelings
Korason - Heart
Agradesi - Appreciation
Madaña - Getting together
Kariñu - Affection
Kariñosu - Affectionate
Kontratta - Date

Do you have a date?
Guaha Kontratta-mu?

Do you want to go out on a date?
Kao malagu hao ya ta kontratta ya ta huyong?

Love potion - **Atgimat**

He was bewitched by her beauty.
Inatgimat ni bunita-ña.

She was bewitched by his looks.
Inatgimat ni bunitu-ña.

Love is blind - **Bachet na guinaiya**
Jealous - **Ekgo'**
I'm jealous over my spouse. - **Hu ekgu'i i asagua-hu**
Nobody loves me – **Ni hayi gumuaiya yu'**
I will never love you – **Ni ngai'an na hu guaiya hao**
Nobody loves me at all – **Ni hayiyi gumuaiya hao**
I don't like anyone at all - **Ni hayiyi ya-hu na taotao**

No matter how much you may call, I wont answer.
Ni taimanu agang-mu ti un ineppe.

No matter what you do, I won't like it.
Ni hafa un chogue, ti bai hu malagu'.

I miss you.
Hu alaisen hao. or
Mampos yu mahalang nu hagu.

Kiss me - **Chiku yu**
Hug me - **Toktok yu**
Special words - **Espesiat na palabra siha**
I'm really happy we've met - **Sen magof yu na umasodda' hit**
You're delicious (yes, this is really used) - **Mange hao** –
I worried a lot about you - **Mampos yu chathinasso pot hagu**
I need you - **Hu nisisita hao**
I can't live without you - **Ti siña yu mula'la sin hagu**
Don't break my heart - **Munga mayamak este korason-hu**

You fill my heart with joy
Hagu munabula minagof i korason-hu

Come closer to me
Na ihot hao magi giya guahu or **Sigi magi giya guahu**

Would you like to dance with me?
Malagu hao bumaila yan guahu?

Will you marry me? - **Kao siña un asagua yu?**

Articles

In the Chamorro language, there really isn't much use for an indefinite artcle in conversation. However, when used it is actually gender neutral as masculine/feminine articles were not present prior to Spanish colonization. In any case the article un is used to identify an object if necessary:

un lata - a can
un palao'an - a woman
un peskadot - a fisherman

In Spanish, there would be the distinction between genders in using un, una, unos, unas, etc.

Definite articles in Chamorro are also limited to i, si, and as. The placement of i before most nouns and verbs and depending upon placement within the sentence, it can affect the spelling of the following word.

uchan - rain
i ichan - the rain

guma siha - houses
i gima siha - the houses

Si is commonly used in reference to people and placed in front of names:

Si Teresita - Teresita
Si Raina - The Queen
Si Yu'us - God

As is typically used before names of places or things and can sometimes be used in referring to someone in the third person for describing a specific characteristic:

As Tapochau (name of a mountain)
I kaduka as Ana - Ana "the idiot"

I chelu-mu as Ton - Your brother Tony

As can also be used in identifying authorship i.e.:

Written by Juan Babauta
Tinige' as Juan Babauta

9 AROUND THE HOUSE

Chogue i tarea-mu
Do your chores

Chogue i tarea-mu - Do your chores

Take out the trash - **Chule i basula huyong**
Empty the waste bins - **Chuda i basula**
Put a trash bag in the trash can - **Pu'luye botsiyo i sagan basula**

Po'lo i applacha na magagu gi hamper.
Put dirty clothes in the hamper.

Put the clothes in the washer/dryer
Po'lo i magagu gi halom i labadot/makina muna'anglo.

Fold the clothes - **Dopbla i magagu**
Iron the shirt/pants - **Prensa i flanela/katsunes**
Do the laundry - **Fagasi i magagu**
Dry the clothes - **Nafan'anglo i magagu**
Do the dishes - **Fagasi i na'yan**
Dry the dishes - **Nafan'anglo i na'yan**
Don't use the dishwasher - **Chamo na sesetbi i dishwasher**
Feed the dog/cat/fish - **Nachocho i galagu/katu/guihan**
Feed the animals/pets - **Nachocho i ga'ga'**
Bathe the dog - **Na'omak i galagu**
Change the water in the fish tank - **Tulaika i hanom i guihan**
Change the litter box - **Tulaika i sagan i katu**
Walk the dog - **Nafanmokkat i galagu**
Let the cat out - **Nahuyung i katu**

Pick up all the stuff off the floor.
Hokka i kosas-mu gi hilo' satge

Dust (telling someone to dust) - **Saosao i petbos**
Vaccuum the house - **Vaccuum i halom guma**

Sweep the floor - **Bale satge**
Mop the floor - **Lampasu i satge**

Take the rug outside and beat it.
Chule i atfombra yan tantan gi sanhiyong.

Scrub the toilet/shower
Guesgues i kemmon/sagan umo'mak

Clean the bathroom - **Na'gasgas i halom kommon**
Help your brother/sister - **Ayuda i chelu-mu lahi/palao'an**
Cook - **Na'la'gu**
Barbecue the meat - **Tunu i katne**

Clear the table
Nagasgas i lamasa or **Hatsa i sintada** (clear dishes)

Wipe the table/shelf - **Saosao i lamasa/tapblita**
Set the table - **Planta i na'yan**
Water the flowers - **Rega i flores**
Mow the lawn - **Utut i cha'guan**

Pull the weeds - **Bokbok i chaguan**
Put fertilizer - **Pu'luye' ha'bono** or **Habonuye'**
Turn on the sprinklers - **Nakalamtin i fanregayan**
Wash the car - **Fa'gasi i kareta**
Clean the inside of the car - **Nagasgas i halom kareta** (detailing)
Put the dishes away - **Po'lo siha i na'yan**

I already did it - **Esta hu cho'gue/Esta munayan**
I'm about to do it - **Esta para bai cho'gue**
I'll do it tomorrow - **Bi cho'gue agupa/Bai hu cho'gue agupa**

Do it now, tomorrow might not come.
Chogue pa'go, sa ti u fatto agupa.

Work smarter, not harder (lit: do it right, don't rush)
Namaolek i checho-mu, munga mapakiao.

Do you need any help? - **Kao un nesesita ayuda?**

A quick look at conjugation...

We need more food - **Tanesesita mas nengkanno'**
Do we need more food? - **Kao tanesesita mas nengkanno'?**

I need to go grocery shopping.
Hu nesesita para bi hanao ya bai famahan nengkanno.
(**lateria** - canned goods)

You need to go grocery shopping.
Un nesesita para un hanao para un famahan nengkanno.

Ta nesesita na ta hanao para ta fanmahan nengkanno.
We need to go grocery shopping.

The difference in referencing the third person:

Debi di ufanhanao ya u fanmamahan nengkanno.
They need to go grocery shopping (a neutral, general statement)

Debi di siha ufanhanao ya u fanmamahan nengkanno.
They need to go grocery shopping (i.e. "I'm not going to do it for them!" A sarcastic remark)

I Palabras i Saina - A Parent's Words

Wake up - **Fakmatta**
It's time to get up - **Kahulo'** or **Fakmatta pa'go**
Make your bed - **Arregla i kama-mu**
Wash your face - **Fagasi i mata-mu**
Brush your teeth - **Guesgues i nifen-mu**
Take a shower - **O'mak**
Come eat - **Maila ya un cho'cho**

Do the dishes - **Chogue na'yan**
Do the laundry - **Famagasi**
Your room is a mess - **Machalapun i kuatto-mu**
Clean your room - **Nagasgas i kuatto-mu**
Did you clean your room? - **Kao un na gasgas i kuatto-mu?**

Pick up your things off the floor.
Hokka i kosas mu gi hilo satge.

Eat everything on your plate.
Kanno todo i nengkanno gi platu-mu.

Don't talk with your mouth full.
Munga kumuentos yanggin motmot i pachot-mu.

Close your mouth when you chew.
Huchong i pachot mu yanggin chumochocho' hao.

You weren't raised by wolves (animals).
Ti ga'ga hao pumoksai.

Don't talk back - **Cha'mu fan o'ope**
You're going to get hit - **Siempre masaolak hao**
I'm your parent, not your friend - **Saina-mu yu, ti amiga-mu yu**
This is for your own good - **Este para i minaolek-mu**

It hurts me more than it hurts you.
Addenña i puti-hu ki i puti-mu.

You must respect your elders - **Debi di un respeta i manamku**
Don't hit your sister/brother - **Munga ma naputi i chelu-mu**

If you hit an elder, your fingers will be crippled.
Kumu un inbeste i amko-mu siempre hao hakku.

Stop whining - **Basta di un kati/kaduku**
Stop making faces - **Basta di un atan ti maolek**
Don't roll your eyes - **Chamu rolrolyu i mata-mu**

If you keep rolling your eyes, one day they won't stop
Sigi ha di un rolyu i mata mu, un diha siempre sigi ha
kumililok i atadok-mu   or
Sigi ha di un rolyu i matamu, sa un dia siempe ti pumara
rumolyu i mata-mu.

Stop fighting - **Basta mumu**
Stop yelling - **Basta mesalao**
One more word! - **Un palabras ha!**
Don't be disrespectful - **Munga dumisatentu**

If I have to tell you one more time, you're gonna get it.
Otro biahi na bai sagani hao, siempre u na pangpang hao.

Did you brush your teeth? - **Kao un guesgues i nifen mu?**
Did you shower/take a bath? - **Kao umo'mak hao?**
Did you say your prayers? - **Esta hao manaitai?**
Go to bed - **Sigi bai katre-mu**
Go to sleep - **Sigi ya un maigu**

You have to get up early tomorrow.
Debi di un fatmatta taftaf agupa.

Sweet dreams - **Mames na guinifi**
Good night - **Buenas noches or Maolek na puengi**

If you raise your children to be ravens, they'll peck your eyes out.
Baba piniksaimu ni patgon-mu siempre humuyong inimbeste hao/akkontra hao.
(Lit: If you raise your children badly, they'll hurt you/turn against you)

You act like your ashamed but you're shameless anyway.
Mamahlao hao nu i taimamahlao-mu.

Spare the rod, spoil the child.
Munga mampos gusto gi patgon mu,
sa siempre humuyong desgusto.
(Lit: If you spoil your kids, they'll turn out to be disgusting)

Discipline your kids well.
Arreglan maolek i patgon-mu.

Stop acting stupid, or you're gonna end up stupid (insane).
Basta di un famakaduku sa u timoña siempre atmariao hao.

Note: While some of the phrases may appear harsh, it is not unusual to hear such statements in the midst of "Old School" Chamorro parenting.

Trastes Kusina – Kitchen Items

abrelata - can opener
bandeha - platter
basu - glass
batea - a large wash pan, wash tub
chachak pitsa - pizza cutter
chareran cha - tea kettle
charera yan hara - pitcher
estante - cabinet
estanten na'yan nengkanno - spice rack
etses - grater
famikayan - chopping board
foggon ilektresida - electric range
foggon gas - gas stove
grifu - faucet
gua'hen chada' - spatula
guesgues na'yan yan habon - brillo & dishwashing liquid
hafyen sentada - placemat
kahon ais - refrigerator
kalahi -big pot
kanastran numa'tuho' na'yan - dish drainer
kana' saosao kannai - hand & dish towel rack
koladot numa'tuho' - colander
kuchala - spoons
kucharon - ladle
la'uya - pot
labadot - sink
lamasa - table
lata - can/canister
latan basula / tampe-ña - trash can / cover
machete, punat - bolo-knife, dagger
makinan mama'tinas kafe -coffee maker
makinan mambatte - mixer
manu/manon mamadda' titiyas - corn/flour rolling pin
mulinon gollai - vegetable grinder
mulinon katne yan eskomme - meat & corn grinder
platitu - saucer
platu - plate

platon karai - plastic plate
pusuelu - coffee cups
aosao na'yan kannai - dish and hand towels
setbeyeta - napkins
sahguan ansopbla - left over food container
sahguan pan - bread box
se'se' - knife
siya - chair
takuren kafe/ chareran kafe - coffee kettle
tasa - cup
tason - bowl
tampen-ña - its cover
tenidot-fork

10 SPECIAL OCCASIONS AND SAYING GOODBYE

Gi Plasan Batkon Aire
At the Airport

Gi ofisiu na ofisina - At the post office

How much is it to mail this box to Saipan?
Kuanto baliña este na kaheta yanggin bai hu na hanao para Saipan?

How long does it take for a box to arrive in California?
Kuanto tiempo para u tinaka ni para u fatto este na kaheta guato giya California?

I want to send my sister some senbei and guyuria.
Malago yu para bai hu nahanagui i chelu palao'an palu senbei yan guyuria.

Is the box heavy? **Kao makkat i kaheta?**
How much does it weigh? **Kuanto i minakkat-ña?**
How big is the box? **Kuanto dinangkulo-ña i kaheta?**
Let's find out. **Po'lo ya ta sodda'.**

What time does the Post office open?
Ki ora para uma'baba i ofisiu na ofisina?

What time does the Post Office close?
Ki ora para uma'huchom i ofisiu na ofisina?

Are you open on Saturday? **Kao mababa este an Sabalu?**

Is it okay to mail food?
Maolek ha ya bai hu na hanao nengkanno'?

Is it okay to mail perfume?
Maolek ha ya bai hu na hanao i paopao?

It is not okay to mail flammable materials.
Ti siña u despacha i maninila na materiat.

Make sure that you packed the box yourself.
Adahi na ti hago pumaketi i kaheta-mu.

Did a stranger come into contact with the box?
Kao i estrangheru matto ya ha ke'tungo i kaheta'mu?

No, there is only snacks from Saipan in the box.
Ahe, puru ha mirinda gi halom i kaheta ni ginen Saipan.

That will be $40. Will you be paying with cash, check, or credit today?
Pot todo, kuarenta pesos. Kao para un apasi pa'go kas, chek, pot kreditu?

Here you go. **Pues esta** or **Maolek ha.**
Okay, have a nice day. **Maolek ha, puedi bonitu i ha'ane-mu.**

Kasamentu
Wedding

Congratulations on your wedding!
Komplimento i kasamento-mu!

What's the bride's name?
Hayi na'an-ña i nobia?

Her name is Igniacia.
Si Ignacia na'an-ña.

What's the groom's name?
Hayi na'an-ña i nobio?

His name is Enrique.
Si Enrique na'an-ña.

What time is the ceremony?
Ki ora i umakkamu?

It's at eight in the morning at San Roque.
Alas ocho gi egga'an gi San Roque.

What's the name of that bridal song?
Hafa na'an-ña ayu na kantan nobia?

"Arise Bride". Let's sing it together.
"Nobia Kahulo". Nihi ta hita kumanta.

Happy Anniversary!
Biba kumpleaños umassagua!

Nihi ta fan hanao para i gima Yu'us
Let's go to church

Let's pray
Nihi ta fan manayuyut.

What time is the rosary?
Ki ora i lisayu?

What time is the party?
Ki ora i gipot?

What are we going to make/prepare?
Hafa para ta fa'tinas?

Desde pa'go para mo'na u sen makkat
From now on life will be more difficult,
i lina'la sa' taigui I ante ni'
Lacking the one who
Muna'fanggagai sastansia todu.
Was the life of all.

An numa' piniti hao taotao
When you hurt somebody,
Nangga ma na' piniti-mu;
Be expecting to be in pain;
Maseha apmaman na tiempo,
For even if it takes time,
U apasi sa' dibi-mu.
Surely you'll pay for the pain you caused.

Taya' mina'lak sin hinemhum.
There is no brightness without darkness.
Taya' tataotao sin anining.
There is no body without its shadow.
Taya' finaitai sin sina'pit.
There is no death without suffering.

Taya' aksion sin rason.
There is no action without reason.

God never sleeps - **Ti mamaigu si Yu'us**

I extend to all of you a big thank you for the support, blessings, and vote of confidence.
Hu ekstetende un dangkolo na si Yu'us ma'ase todos hamyo guini ni man gaige nu i suppottasion, i bendision, yan i botun konfiansa.

Sinisa yan Kuaresma - Ash Wednesday and Lent

As you may or may not know, the majority of Chamorros are Roman Catholic. **Sinisa** marks the start of **Kuaresma**. On **Sinisa**, you have your penitensia to carry out and of course **munga makanno katne an Betnes**! **Ayunat** is required for the more able bodied and healthy while those who have health issues are exempt from doing so. Throughout this season of **Kuaresma**, we look forward to **Semana Santa**. This starts with **Ramos** and it's suggested not to eat meat at all throughout the week.

Semana Santa starts to wrap up with **Huebes Santo**, which includes the washing of the feet ceremony at the **Santa Misa**. Followed by **Huebes Santo** is **Betnes Santo**, **Sabalun Loria**, and finally **Pasgua**.

Bukabulariu - Vocabulary

Sinisa - Ash Wednesday
Kuaresma - Lent
Penitensia (Penance) - Giving up something for Lent
Ayunat - Fasting
Munga makanno katne an Betnes - Don't eat meat on Fridays
Guihan - Fish
Katne - Meat
Santa Misa - Holy Mass
Semana Santa - Holy Week
Ramos - Palm Sunday
Huebes Santo - Shroud Thursday
Betnes Santo - Good Friday
Sabalun Loria - Holy Saturday
Pasgua – Easter
Happy Easter – Felis Pasgua

Huebes Santo yan i Matuna na Magagon Jesukristo
Holy Thursday and The Holy Shroud

Huebes Santo is a profound and elaborate day which is comparable to the Easter Vigil mass on Sabalun Loria. On Huebes Santo, Jesukristo offers himself as the Passover Victim, the ultimate self-sacrifice, a tradition in which is followed by the ordination of priests for the sake of service and humility. The Last Supper served as Jesukristo's farewell to the Apostles and the last time He points out those who betray and deny Him. On Huebes Santo the Santa Misa is marked by a special ceremony, i mafagasi i patas. Anai si Jesukristo ha fagasi i addeng i man disipulu, this also reflected the meaning of feet that is still believed in the Middle East today.

To show one's feet by placing them on furniture, touching one's feet to another person or any object of significance, and displaying your soles to another is a great sign of disrespect as the feet are considered to be the filthiest part of the body in most, if not all, Middle Eastern cultures. The action of Jesukristo was an act of humility as to wash the feet of the Apostles was an act of lowering oneself for the service and care for your fellow human being. In the Santa Misa, 12 people are chosen to have their feet washed by the pale or bishop, representing the 12 Apostles. This also is a reflection of the Jewish ritual cleaning of one's home in preparation of the Passover.

This is also the day of the 'Chrism Mass' where the blessing of the Oil of Chrism used for Bautismo and Konfetmasion takes place. Tha Santa Misa for Huebes Santo is celebrated in an evening mass because Passover begins at sundown. This is the expression of the importance Yu'us places on selfless service and humility. This day also offers a similar celebration of Passover in which certain foods such as lamb and unleavened bread are made according to the book of Exodus. The Passover Seder commemorates the connection of Christianity and Judaism. It's neither meant to be a re-enactment of i Uttimo na Sena nor an official Jewish service or rite. However, the significance is placed upon recalling history in the study and practice of religion. This first day of the Easter Triduum is a day where you can begin abstinence of meat and fasting, but some choose to officially begin Friday.

Bukabulariu - Vocabulary

Huebes Santo - Holy Thursday
Sabalun Loria - Holy Saturday
I mafagasi i patas - washing of the feet
Anai si Jesukristo ha fagasi i addeng i man disipulu - Jesus washes the feet of His Disciples
Jesukristo - Jesus Christ
Santa Misa - Holy Mass
Pale - Priest
Bautismo - Baptism
Konfetmasion - Confirmation
Yu'us - God
I Uttimo na Sena - The Last Supper

Ramos - Palm Sunday

Ramos is the sixth and last Sunday of Kuaresma and start of Semana Santa. Part of the ceremonies of the day are the bendision of the patma, the lukao, and the Santa Misa which includes the Passion. On the attat, branches of patma are placed between the danges instead of flores ordinarily used. The pale sprinkles the patma with pila agua bendita, passes the insensio over them, and, after another tinayuyut, passes the patma bendita about.

When you want to bless a house, the patma is used after it has had time to dry and taken out of it's shape if it's a cross before burning.

Bukabulariu – Vocabulary

Ramos - Palm Sunday
Kuaresma - Lent
Semana Santa - Holy Week
bendision - blessing
patma - palm
patma bendita - blessed palm
lukao - procession
Santa Misa - Holy Mass
attat - altar
danges - candles
flores - flowers
pale - priest
pila agua bendita - holy water
insensio - incense
tinayuyut – prayer

Felis Nabidat yan Felis Año Nuebo
Merry Christmas and a Happy New Year

As many Chamorros know, using "Felis Pasgua" for Merry Christmas has been commonplace in the Marianas. This saying is actually incorrect as "Pasgua" is Easter, not Christmas. This comes from the Spanish "Feliz Pascua" for Happy Easter and "Feliz Navidad" for Merry Christmas.

Merry Christmas
Felis Nabidat

Merry Christmas to you all!
Felis Nabidat para todos hamyo!

Happy New Year
Felis Año Nuebo

Fanmatto' Manheñgge
(Adeste Fidelis/O Come All Ye Faithful)
This is not a direct translation from the English "O Come All Ye Faithful" but this is the Chamorro version sung during Christmastime and in the same melody.

Fanmatto' Manheñgge
Fata i minagof
Fanmatto, fanmatto giya Belen.

Atan i Patgon,
Rai Anghet siha;
Tañgiñgi ta'adora,
Tañgiñgi ta'adora,
Tañgiñgi ta'adora,
Si Jesus.

Ilek-ña i anghet nu i pastot siha,
Estague i Kristo giya Belen,
Gi sagan gaga, chatsaga, taigima

Tañgiñgi ta'adora,
Tañgiñgi ta'adora,
Tañgiñgi ta'adora,
Si Jesus.

I malak na ina, Lahen Yu'us Tata,
Humuyong sen Taotao achaiguata.
O yiniusan Dikiki na Patgon.
Tañgiñgi ta'adora,
Tañgiñgi ta'adora,
Tañgiñgi ta'adora,
Si Jesus.

Malañgo i taotao, ti amtiyon esta,
lao matto si Yu'us ni Yoamte.
Guiya i amot nahomlo yan mames.
Tañgiñgi ta'adora,
Tañgiñgi ta'adora,
Tañgiñgi ta'adora,
Si Jesus.

Gi Plasan Batkon Aire - At the Airport

What time is your flight?
Ki ora ni para un gupu? or
Ki ora i malagu-mu? or
Ki ora hinanao-mu.

I'm scheduled to depart on Flight 777 on United Airlines from Saipan to Tokyo.
Masanganiyu na para biahu gupu gi 777 gi United na batkon aire ginen Saipan para Tokyo.

Where are you flying to? **Para manu guatu ni para un gupu?**

I'm flying back to Florida. **Para bai hu gupu tatte guato Florida.**
Wow, that's a long trip! **Ai, mampos chagu enao na karera!**

Tell me about it. Including layovers, it took me almost 36 hours to get to Saipan!
Hu'u anai, siña sangan enao. Kontodo i para bai fannangga, kana 36 na ora ni para bai hu fatto guato Saipan.

What?! That's too long for me! That's why I never travel.
Hafa?! Mampos anakko enao para guahu. Ayu, na taya nai kumarera yu.

I started in Florida, then flew to New Jersey, then Hong Kong, then Guam, and finally Saipan.
Hu tutuhon ginen Florida, pues gumupayo' guato New Jersey, pues Hong Kong, pues guato Guam, yan gi uttimo guato Saipan.

Thank you for coming from such a long distance.
Si Yu'us ma'ase pot i finato-mu sa mampos anakko i distansia.

It was so nice to see you again. **Magof yu sa huli'e hao ta'lo.**

Next time, we're going to have an even bigger fiesta.
Otro biahe, tana mas dangkolo i fiesta.

126

I'll miss you so much. **Siempre mahalang yu nu hagu.**

I'll miss you too. Be sure to call me.
Guahu lokkue siempre mahalang yu. Na siempre na un agang yu.

I'll write you emails more often. And don't forget to call mom when you land.
Sesso siempre bai hu tuge'i hao email. Ya cha'mu maleffa na ti un agang si Na yanggin matto hao guatu.

Travel safe! **Safo! Mona gi karera-mu.**

Where is immigration?
Mangge i immigrasion? or
Manu nai gaige i immigrasion?

Where is the line for customs? **Mangge i filan i reditu?**

Where is the baggage claim?
Amanu nai gaige ni siña un chule i maleta-mu?

Is the flight delayed or on time?
Kao ma detieni este na karera pat ta'lulo' i ora?

Due to severe weather, the flight has been cancelled.
Pat i mampos baba i tiempo, ma kansela i ginipu.

Is there a long layover in Hong Kong?
Hafa mohon anakko para ta fan man nangga giya Hong Kong?

Good, because I want to go shopping there.
Maolek, sa malago yu humanao ya bai hu famahan gue.

Did you pack everything you needed?
Kao todo un paketi i un nisisita?

Did you forget anything? **Kao taya maleffa-mu?**

Do you have anything to declare?
Kao guaha mas para un deklara?

I wish I could take some parrot fish with me.
Hu diseseha mohon na siña bai ke'chule i palaksi na guihan.

Do you think I could pack it with dry ice in a cooler?
Hafa mohon siña bai hu paketi este ni angglo na ais?

Yes, but you're running out of time. Next time, plan ahead.
Hunggan, lao kalan taya esta tiempon-mu. Otro biahe planeha kontiempo.

I love you.
Hu guaiya hao.

Goodbye!
Adios!

Chamorro-English Glossary

a'a - open mouth
a'ada - mimicker, mocker
a'adahi - guard, caretaker
a'akonseha - adviser
a'amte - healer
a'aposta - gambler
a'arekla - repairman
a'atte - magician, clairvoyant
a'ayuda - helper
a'baba - feeble-minded
a'ñao - overpower
abahu - cleared land
abak - lost, astray
abalansa – balance
abale - intercourse
abandonao - abandoned
abas - guava
abeha - bee, honeybee
abiba - incite, inspire
abietto - open
abirigua - to question, interrogate
abisa - advise, notify
abok – friend (older Chamorro term)
abona - take sides (in a discussion, etc.)
abrasu – hug
Abrit - April
achago - distance
achakma' - shacking up, having an affair
achataotao - peer, people of equal age
acho' - rock
achom - sneeze
achoti - seeds for coloring rice (hineksa' agaga')
adahi - caution
adda' - ridicule, copy
addak - to hit, strike hard
addeng - feet, leg
addet - strict, severe
adespatta - disconnect
addo' - sea grapes
adibina - to prophesize, foretell
adimas - rather than

adingan - converse, talk
adinganiyi - to intercede for someone
adingu - departure
adios - good-bye
adora - adore, worship
adotgan - hole, tunnel
adotna - to decorate or beautify
adotteru - adulterer
adu - to spy on, watch, peep
aduana - taxes
a'duko' - idiot
adulisensia - adolescence
adumidide - little by little
afabilidat - friendliness, courtesy
afa'fa - armpit
afagao - husky voice
afa'maolek - to collabrate (group work)
afekta - to affect
afitma - to affirm
aflitu - fry afloha - slacken, loosen
afuera - keep out
afuetsao - obligation
aga' - banana (ripe)
aga'ga' - neck
agaga' - red
agaliya - stretcher for carrying someone
agang - call
agaode - to cross one's legs
agapa' - right direction
agara - grab, claim
agguas - infant mullets (fish)
agila - eagle
agon - starchy food
Agosto - August
ago'te - shake or hold hands
agradesi - appreciate
agua bendita - Holy water
aguaguati - fight, disagree
agululumi - to gang up, band together
agumento - argument
agupa' - tomorrow
agupan'na - day after tomorrow
ahe' - no ahu - coconut pudding

ai - ouch, wow aire - air
akague - left direction
akgang - loud
akidi - so much time passing
akka' - bite
aklara - to declare
alageta - avocado
alamle - cable, wire
alapat - parallel
alileng - cone shell
alu - baracuda (fish)
aluda - groupers (fish)
alula - hurry
amariyu - yellow
amkko' - old
amot - medicine
amot gapotulu - hair spray
amotsa - breakfast, lunch
anakko' - long
angglo - dry
aniyu - ring for finger
anonas - custard or sugar apple
antigu - ancient, primitive
antios - eyeglasses
años - age, years
apaga - shoulder
a'paka' - white
apasi - pay
aposta - bet, wager
applacha' - dirty
arekla - fix, repair
arina - flour
asagua - marry
asagua - spouse
Asaina - Lord, God
asiga - salt
asukat - sugar
asuli - eel (salt or fresh water)
atadok - eyes
atan - look at
atdao - sun
ates - sweetsop, sugar apple
atmangao - spotted sea crab

atmayas - oatmeal
atopulang - sea crab
atrasao - late
attamobet - automobile (this is mostly used in Guam, not elsewhere)
atuhong laggua - parrotfish (very large)
atulai - mackerel
atuli - porridge
ayao - borrow
ayu - that
ayuda - help, assist
ayuyu - coconut crab

ba' - to crawl on hands and knees
ba'ba' - stunted growth
baba - bad baba - open
bababa' - thick-headed, stupid
babali - eyelash, eyelid
baballe - sweeper (person)
baban boteya - bottle opener
babn lata - can opener
babarias - foolishness, stupidity
baberu - bib
babuen halom tano' - wild pig/boar
babui - pig
bach - badge
bachet - blind
badu - hunch-backed
bafa - buffer
bagamondo - moocher, loafer
bagon - salty seafood
baha - to bend down
bahakke - work clothes
bahia - bay, harbor
baias - bias baila - dance
bailadot(m)/bailadora (f) - dancer
baka - cow
bakante - free time
bakasion - vacation
baketa - to beat up
baketasu - hurt, beat up
bakiya - young cow, calf
bakulu - crutch
bakuna - vaccination

bala - bullet
balaku - pig(boar/male)
balas - a whip or switch
balate' - sea cucumber
balensiana - cooked Spanish rice
balenten pachot - someone who likes to brag
balentia - a fight to the finish
bali - worth, value
balibagu - a lazy person
balisa - suitcase
balua - to value
banda - side, corner
bando - to look for or shout for someone
bangheliu - the Gospel
bangko - stool or bench
banidat - vanity
banidosu/a - show off
banko - bench or bank
baobao - a plump or bloated person
baotismo - Baptism
bapot lumi'of - submarine
baranka - rugged terrain
baratu - cheap, inexpensive
baratura - on sale
bariu - district bas - bus
basnak - fall down
basta - stop, enough
basta hiya' - no kidding
bastos - rough
basu - cup, drinking glass
basula - trash
batangga - any form of sled
batatas - potatoes
bataya - battle
batayon - battalion
batbaru - bold, wild
batbudu - hairy
batko - ship, submarine
batkon - balcony
batkon aire - airplane
batkon aire - airplane, helicopter, glider
batkon gera - battleship
batkon laya - sailboat

batsa - raft
baya' - fed up
bañu - shower, bath
be'i - bandage
bebe' - vagina
bela - wake (funeral)
bende - sell
bendisi - to bless
bentaha - benefit
bentana - window
bente - twenty
besbes - to sizzle (cooking)
bespiran Añu Nuebu - New Year's Eve
bestido - dress
betbu - the word of God
betde - green
betdugu - executioner
beteranu - veteran
betmehu - blonde, light-featured/skinned
Betnes - Friday
betso - verse
biaheru - traveler
biahi - time
biatu - blessed
Biblia - Bible
bibu - fast, hurried
bida - do, act
biha - grandmother, old woman
bihu - grandfather, old man
biktimu - victim
biktoria - victory
bilembines - star apple
bileng - high (substance use)
binaba - foolishness
binadu - deer
binakle - vinegar
binila - bloated (belly)
binilachu - drunkenness
binubu - anger
bira - turn
birada - corner
birenghenas - eggplant
bisikleta - bicycle

bisita - visit, visitor
biskuchu - biscuit
bisnes - business
blanko - throw
bo'bo' - spring water
boksion - pale, deathlike
bokungo' - cave
bola - ball, ball game
bomban guafi - fire extinguisher
boten layak - sailboat
boti - boat
botsa - pocket, put something in pocket
boñelos - doughnut
brabu - healthy
buente - maybe, perhaps
buenu - good
bula - lots of, full
bulachu - drunk
bumisita - visited
bumobola - playing ball
bunita - fusilier fish (large)
bunita - pretty
bunitu - handsome, nice
bunmuchachu - hard-working
buruka - noise
buteti - puffer fish
butsiyu - sack

cha - tea
cha'mu - don't
cha'lak - squirrelfish
cha'ot - allergic
chabai - to resist
chacha' - fussy, choosy
Cha Cha - Chamorro-Latin dance
chachaga' - thigh
chachak - saw
chachatlamen - opponent
chachalamcham - stutterer
chalamlam - twinkle, blink
chada - egg
chaddek - fast
chafleg - to be dying, gravely ill

chagi - try
chago' - far
chaguan tasi - seaweed
chaka - rat
chakchak manana - dawn, daybreak
chalan - road
chalek - laugh
chanda - to nudge (as in elbow s.o.)
chandiha - watermelon
chansa - chance
chaochao - rough
charera - kettle
chatanmak - morning (before dawn)
chatao - selfish, egotistical
chatge - laugh at someone
chat'hinenggue - superstition
chat'hula - to swear falsely, to perjure
chat'ilo - hard-headed, stubborn
chatli'e' - to hate, scold, nag
chatli'iyon - hatred, hostility
chatmata - poor eyesight
chatpago - ugly
chatpayon - wicked, infamous
chatsaga – difficult
chatta' - hardly, barely
chebot - fat, fleshy
chechet - call attention to
chechihet - benevolent
checho - boundary
chefla - to whistle
che'lu - sibling
chetan - to be in error
chetnot - wound, sore, pain
chetnudan - wounded
chetton - stick to, stuck
chi - end or border
chiba - goat
chicheriko - vain or dolled-up
chichula - capricious
chiguet - tweezers
chihit - to draw closer or affectionate
chiku - kiss
chili - penis

chilong - proportionate
chinadek - speed
chinatao - selfishness, greed
chinatli'e - spite
chinema - temperance, abstinence
chinema maisa - self-control
chinetan - misunderstanding
chinina - shirt
chisme - slander
chispas - spark
cho'cho' - work
cho'gue - do, perform
chocho - eat
chomma' -forbid
chonnek - push
chopchop - suck
chorisos - sausage
chotda - banana
chotda betde - green bananas
chubasko - swell
chugha - even
chugo' - juice, pus
chukan - to wallow
chukulati - chocolate
chule' - take
chule' - take, bring
chule' pot banida - to take for granted
chupa - smoke a cigarette; cigarette
chupon - pale, sallow

dadau - sharp, keen
daddek - young coconut
dado - dice
dagan - buttocks, hips
daggan - buttocks
daggao - throw
dagi - lie
dagon haya - yam
dagu - yam
dagua - sun-burned
dai - friend
dakon - liar
dakot - to beat over one's head

dalak - accompany, follow
dalalai - slender, skinny
dalalak - to imitate, follow
dama - checkers (the game)
da'ma'gas - thumb, toes
Damenggo - Sunday
danche - to find,
dandan - music
dangkolo - large
daña' - combined, be together
dañao - to damage or hurt
dañgue - timid, cowardly
dañgues - candle
dañguis - rubber, resin
dañgse - to smear, grease
dañgson - sticky
dañoso - detrimental
dasai - to shave or shear
datilis - date palm (tree)
debana - to cut into slices
debanada - thin slice
debidi - must, have to
debit - weak, feeble, haggard, milquetoast
debotsia - divorce
debosion - devotion, piety
deboto - pious, devout, religious
debuena boluntad - of free will, voluntarily
debuetta - compensation, amends
dedego - heel (of one's foot)
dedsiplina - discipline
dei - friend
defekto - fault, blemish
defensot - protector, guardian
defiende - to support with proof, defend
definision - definition
dego - to tip-toe
deha - to crouch
delikao - tender
deletrea - to spell, spell out
delikadesa - delicacy, precision
delisioso - delicious
demanda - to demand or ask promptly
demanadot/akusadot - plaintiff (legal/law)

demasiao - superfluous
demonio - demon
dentro - within
de'on - pinch, pinch, tweak
dependiente - subordinate, lower in rank or position
deposita - to deposit
deposito - warehouse
depotsiha - naturally
derechos/aduana - fees, customs
derepente - sudden, abruptly
deroga - diminish, withdraw
desabrido - tasteless, unpleasant
desaguadero - sewer system
desampara - to desert, forsake, abandon
desaprueba - to denounce, condemn
desareglao - disorder
desase - to ruin, destroy
desatento/a - disrespectful
desatiende - to neglect
desbetga - to injure or violate
desde - since, from
desde ki - ever since
desecha/yuti - to throw away
desembatka - to disembark
desempeña - to provide for
desendiente - descendant
desente - clean, neat, pleasing
desenteresao - disinterested
deseo - choice
desesperao - desperate, hopeless
desfaborable - ominous, evil
desfigura - to disfigure
desfila - to pass by
desgrasia - disgrace, disaster
deshase - to ruin
deshereda - to disinherit
deshilachas - to unravel
deshonesto - indecent, impure
deshonra - to dishonor
deside - to decide
Desiembre - December
desietto - desert
desimat - decimal

desision - decision
deskalintao - stale, tasteless
deskansa - rest
deskarao - insolent, shameless
deskatga - to unload, discharge
deskolorao - deathlike, pale
deskonfiansa - mistrust, suspicion
deskubre - to discover
deskuenta - to withdraw
deskuida - carelessness
desminuye - to decimate
desmonta - to clear/cut down trees
desokupao - unoccupied
despabila - to awaken to reason
despacha - to disband
desparadot - trigger (gun)
despasiu - slow
despega - to peel or remove
despensa - forgive
despetdisia - to squander, waste
desprebenido - unprepared, unready
despresia/o - to deprecate, disdain
despues di - after, later
despunta - cut off point
destempla - to be out of tune (music)
destilado - banish or expel, send into exile, outcast
destilipas - to gut
destina - to determine, designate
destinao - fateful
destino - destiny
destrosa - annihilate
detetmine - to determine
detiene - to hold back, detain
dia - day
diamante - diamond
diario - daily
dibatde - free
dibe - debt, due, owing someone
dibetsion - diversion, entertainment
dibettido - joyous, happy
dibide - divide
dibidiyon - divisible
dibino - fortune teller

dibision - division, partition
dibuho - plan, drawing
dicha - luck
dichoso - fortunate, lucky
didefiende - advocate
dideskubre - witty, clever, ingenious
didibe - to be in debt
didinag - parasite
i didirihe - guidance
didok - steep slope
dies - ten
difende - defend
difensot - defender
diferensia - difference
diferente - different
diferentes - diverse
difikultad/minapot - difficulty
dikike - small
diksionario - dictionary
dikta - to dictate, orate
diles - to excel
dilok - upside-down
dilubio - deluge
dimalas - misfortune, bad luck
dinagi - denial, deceit
dinagñgas - bald spot on one's head
dinalalak - imitation
dinamo elecktrisida - electric dryer
dinaña - mixture, blend
dinañai - turnout, siding
dinanche - just, truthful
dinebit - imperfection, weakness
dineklara - to declare
dineko - growth, increase
dinemanda - lawsuit
dinemo - to punch
dinesanima - depressed, melancholic
dineskansa - leisure
dineskuida - oversight, neglect
dingu - depart, leave behind
dinichoso - balm; blessedness
dinigrido - black and blue, ashy
dinira - endurance, to continue

diñga - twins, double
diñgo - abandon, leave, desert
dipende - depend
direkto - direct straight
dirite - to dissolve
disanima - to dishearten
disatiende - to snub
disatma - to disarm
disimula - to keep secret, conceal
diskutpa - to justify, excuse
diskutso - formal speech
disgusta - disgust
dispabilao - tact
dispara - to fire a gun
disparateria - blasphemy
dispensa - to excuse
dispone - to prepare
distansia - distance
distinto - distinctive
distraido - distracted
distrito - district
dobla - to bend, fold
doblan-magago - crease
dochon - to penetrate
dochon na inatan - to give an intense stare
dodolle - being overpowered
doga - leather shoe
do'gas - sea shell
dogñgos - burnt, dry
dokdok - seeded breadfruit
dole - to humble oneself
domina - to govern, rule
dommo' - punch
donne' - chilli pepper
donseya - maiden
dopbla - bend, fold
dos - two
dose - twelve
dosuk - to pierce, stab
dreya - dredge
draiba - drive, driver
du'an - wart
duda - doubt

dudok - to buckle/strap on
dudoso - doubtful
dudus - show-off, flirty, too much
duendes - elves, small ghosts
dulok - perforate, hypodermic needle
dumaña - to include
dumeskarada - to show off or flaunt
duranten - during
duru - hard, fast
dulalak - chase, pursue

ebaba - low, lowly
ebangelio - gospel
ebita - to avoid
echong - bent, crooked
echoñgña - side
echung - to distract
eda - soil
edad - age
edas - stage
eduka - to educate
edukasion - education
egaga - to inspect
egga' - watch, observe as spectator
eggo' - jealous
ehe - axis of a cart/wagon
ehekutibo - executive
ehemplo - example
ehetsisio - to drill (military)
ehetsita - to exercise
ehetsito - army, militia (milisia)
ehoñgui - irregular
ekahat - to hunt, pursue
ekibokasion - misunderstanding
eksakto - literal, exact
eksamina - to test, examine
ekspirensia - experience
ekungok - listen
elihe - to elect
embahadot - ambassador
embatka - to embark
embilikeru/a - a meddler, idler
embeste - mutiny, revolt, seizure

embidiosu/a - jealous, envious
emboskada - to ambush
embudo - funnel
emfetmera - nurse
emok - vengeance, retribution
empas - reconcile
empe - half, a piece
empeña - to try, lease
empeñao - zealous
empeño - energy
empeñoso - energetic
emperadot - emperor
empetuoso - irritable
empeya - fat
emplea - to invest, spend time
empleo - office
enagui - look!
enamorao - in love
enao - that
enao guatu - over there
enbano - unnecessarily
en bes di - instead of, in place of
enemigo - enemy
Eneru - January
engaño - trickery, deception
engatsa - to border
enhiniero - engineer
enkaha - to incase
enkatgao - appointed
enlugat di - in place of
eno - blanket
enredadot - slanderer
ensatta - to thread an needle
ensaya - trial, attempt
ensegida - salad
ensenada - cove, bay
ensigidas - right away, immediately
ensina - plum tree
entalo' - between, among
entalu'e - to interfere
entayag - thief
entenadu/a - step-son/step-daughter
enteramente - completely

entre - among, between
entrega - to surrender, yield, sacrifice
entrepulao - miscellaneous
entretanto - in the meantime, however
entre nasion siha - international
eñggrudo - paste
eñguiñ - ungrateful, thankless
epanglao - hunt for crabs
epidemia - plague
epilepsia
epok - to entice
epoka - era
esalao - shouting until hoarse, clamor
eskabeche - fried fish cooked with vegetables, to pickle
eskalefrio - cold shivers
eskama - scales (as on a fish)
eskandalo - scandal
eskandaloso - scandalous
eskapa - to run away
eskapulario - scapular
eskaso - deficiency
eskatlatina - scarlet fever
esklabitud - slavery
esklabo - slave
eskoba - broom
eskopeta - shotgun
eskoplo - chisel
eskribiente - clerk, writer
eskrupuloso/pinalalala - scrupulous
eskuela - school
eskuttot - sculptor
eskusa - to excuse
esfero - sphere, globe
esita - to joke
esitane/fababa - to bluff or deceive
eskina - corner (building)
esmero - eagerness
espada - sword
espanta - to scare away
espantao/luhan - scared
espanto - fright
Españot - Spanish
espedision - expedition

espehos - mirror
espeke - crowbar or lever
espia - look for, spy
espinaso - spine, backbone
espiniya - shank
espiritu - spirit
espitat - hospital
esplika - to explain
esplikaye - to interpret, translate
espoñha - sponge
esposision - exposition
espresa - to express in language
espuelas - spurs
essalao - shout
essena - scene
essitan - joke
esta - okay, ready
estaba - used to
establese - to establish
establesimiento - establishment
estado - territory
estague' - here is
estaka - stake, pole
estampa/litratu - picture
estañgka - to resist, dam
estaño - tin
estao - state of being
estasiones - seasons of the year
este - this
estensibo - estensive
esterit - sterile
estiende - to extend, expand
estila - to distill
estilo - style, fashion
estima - admire
estimao - highly regarded
estomagu - stomach
estoria - story
estotba - to prevent
estotbo - impediment
estrana - annoy, irritate
estranheru - stranger
estraño - unusual

estreyas - stars
estrikto - strict
estropea - to cripple
estudia - to learn
estudiante - student
estudion tataotao - anatomy
estufao - stew
ete/pacha - to touch
etigu - short
etiniñgo - unwise
etmana - nun
etnon - assemblage, gathering
etogo - small in growth
eyak - to imitate or study
eyok - pain from a wound

fa'aila - to accuse (law)
fa'andi - to flatter someone
fa'añao - fearless
fababa - to dupe
fababayon - gullible
faborito - favorite
fabot - favor
fabrika - factory
fabula - fable
fachada - facade, front
fa'chalan - to make room
fache' - mud
fachocho - to work, labor
fadang - federico tree
fa'et - salty
fafababa - swindler, impostor, fraud
fafahan - buyer
fafalago - runner, racer
fahan - buy
faisen - ask
fakae - to share, part
fakanate - to dig a moat or gutter
fakte - catch rain water, tap tree sap
falagu - run
falagui - go and get
famagu'on - children
famalao'an - females

fa'maolek - fix
familia - family
fan - polite particle
fa'na'gue - teach
fanaguiyon - docile, easy to control
fanaitai - read, say prayers
fanala'an - clothes line
fanatugan - hiding place
fandanggo - wedding party
fangana - victory
fanhaluman - filter, passage
fanigue - to distinguish oneself
fanihi - bat
fanmatayan - vital
fanola'an - window
fanomagan - bathtub
fano'makan - shower room, swimming place
fañago - to give birth
fañaki - to rob
fañata'anan - rainy season
fañotsot - to regret
fantasioso - braggart
fata - to expose, display
fata'chong - sit down
fatinas - cook, make
fatinason - possible
fatkiluye - to keep quiet or keep secret
fatmasia - pharmacy
fatoigue - to inspect, overlook
fatpai - to honor
fatso - false
fatta - absent, to lack
fatto - arrive
faya - anchovies
faye - sly, wise, skillful
fe - fidelity, integrity
Febreru - February
fecho - date
fehman - furious, violent
fektos - merchandise, goods
felis - fortunate
felisita - to wish happiness to
fenso - seed, stone

fiadot - surety
fiansa - security, bail
figan - to glow
figura - model, figure
figurin - fashion patterns
fiho - sure
fila - to file
filak - to braid hair
filo - edge
fin - end
fina' - that which is
fina'denne' - hot sauce
finahan - purchase
finakpo - end, conclusion
finalagaihon - indiscretion, slipping
fina'maipe' - made hot, warm up(food)
finamames - sweets
finamta - fertility
fina'tinas - prepare food
fine'na - first
finene'na - first
finilak - basketweaving, braided work
fininut - bundle
fino' - language, speak
finu - smooth
fio - actual
fion - beside, near
fitma - to sign
fitme - strong, firm
flecha - arrow
flete - freight
florero - urn
flores - flower
foda - dull
fo'fo' - to snort
fofona - go ahead!
fogon - stove
fogonero - fireman
fogse - to milk (i.e. a cow)
foggon - stove, barbeque pit
fohmo - damselfish
fo'na - ahead, be first
fondo - foundation, base

fondon tasi - sea floor
fonhayan - to finish
fonton - to belch
forastero - foreign
fotgon - wet
fotma - to form
fotmat - serious, grave
fotmasion - formation
fotnido - sturdy
fottalesa - fertility
fotte - powerful, strong in taste
fottuna - fortune
franela - undershirt
franko - frank, honest, outspoken
frasko - flask
freno - rein
fresa - strawberries
fresko - fresh, cool
frihon - to question, quiz
frion - fool, snob, idiot
frionera - folly
fritadan babui - pork chitterling
fritadan guaka - beef chitterling
fritadan mannok - chicken chitterling
frumeona - to talk silly
fuera de - outside of
fuetsa - power, strength
fuetsao - involuntary
fuette - vigorous, strong
fufatta – insane
fugo' - wring, squeeze
fuhut - to bind lossely
fumiga - to fumigate
fumitme - to become strong
funas - to eradicate, erase, lose color, wither
funda - pillowcase
fundamento - fundamental
funut - to fasten
gabe - to cut or slice
gacha - step on, catch up with
gachai - ax
ga'chong - partner, companion
gada - unripe, uncooked

gadao - grouper fish
gadbo - handsome
gaddo' - wild yam
gade - to snag, get cuaght (clothing)
gadon - to complicate
gafo' - coconut, nearly ripe
ga'ga' - animal, insect, vermin
gago - lazy
gagot - flint stone
gai - have something
gaianimo! - have courage!
gaibale - to be worth
gaibatbas - bearded
gaibittud - energetic
gaifigura - well-built
gaiganansia - profitable
gaige - be present, here, opposite of absent, stative verb
gaihetdan - bothersome
gaihinaso - reasonable
gaihumatsamiento - rebellious
gai'isao - sinner, debtor
gaikulot - multi-colored
gaisensia - common sense
gakumuentos - a babbler, rambler
ga'lagu - dog
galaide' - canoe
galon - gallon
galute - to beat
gamamaisen - inquisitive
ga'man'uga - flatterer
ga'mimo - quarrelsome
gamson - octopus
gana - win
ganadot - winner, champion
ganansia - profit
ganas - desire, appetite
gane - to run aground
ganso - goose
ga'ña - prefer
ga'o - prefer
gaotgan - to choke
gaplaito - to make a fuss
gapotulu - hair

garapatas - tick
garañon -lustful
gaseta - newspaper
gasgas - clean
gasolina - gas
gasta - to spend money
gastadot - extravagance
gasto - expenses
gaston i biahe - travel expenses
gastos - costs
gatano - worldly
gatbo - gorgeous
gatgaras - to gargle
gayetas - cookies
gayo - rooster
gefmanhasso - thoughful
gefpago - charming, pretty
gefsaga - content, comfortable
geftao - big-hearted, kind, magnificent
gekpo - flying, bird
gerra/guerra - war
gerrero/guerrero - warrior
gia - guide
gimen - drink
ginipo - flying
globo - globe
gloria - glory
glorioso - glorious
gobetnadot - governor
gobietna - to govern, manage
gobietnon taotao - democracy
gode - to fasten
gof - very
gofli'e - to love, be loved
gofli'iyon - amiable, lovely
goha - fan, or to blow
gohe - to stoop or bend
golai - vegetable
goleta - schooner
golosina - sweets
goloso/hambiento - greedy, gluttonous
goma - paste
gomgom - to crush

gope - to leap
gopte - to celebrate
gora - bonnet
gosa - to enjoy (food)
gosne - to pull or draw out
gota - to drop
gote - to seize, grip
gotgoreta - water pitcher
gotpe - knock, throw hard
gotpea - to yank
grado - rank, position
gramatika - grammar
granada - pomegranate
granero - granary
graniso - hail
grano - grain
granon ma'is - cornmeal
grasia - grace, thanks
grasioso - clever, inventive
gratifika - to reward
grifo - faucet
griniyete - to chain
griyete - handcuffs
griyos - cricket
guadok - to dig
guafag - mat
guafe - fire
guagse - to peel, shave, scrape
guaguan - expensive
guaguasan - peasant, farmer
guaha - to have
guahe - to dig
guahu - I
guaifi - blow
guaifon - windy
guailaye - useful
guaiya - to love, like
guaiyayon - lovable, sweetheart
guaka - cow
gualafon - full moon
gualo' - farm
guantes - glove
gua'ot - ladder, staircase

guasa - to sharpen
guasang - tonsils
guatda -to guard, keep
guatdia - sentinel
guatnision - to harness an animal
guato - over there (away from speaker)
guayaba - guava
guede - band
guegue - toothpick
gueko - blank (as in paper)
guesgues - to scrape
guha - asthma, pant, cough
guife - to dream, fantasize
guihan - fish
guihen - petticoat
guihi - there, away from person being addressed
guinaiya - ardor, affection
gula - immoderation, gluttony
gulek - grind for grain
guma - house
guma pasahero - inn
guma Yu'us - church
gunus - to sprain
gu'ot - to seize
gupo - to fly
gupot - party
guse'lalalo' - fiery, passionate, easily riled
gusi - fleeting, quickly
gusisiha - immediately
gusto - joy, taste
gutus - to take life

ha'ane - day, daylight
ha'anen gupot - holiday
habao/hakot - to snatch, seize
habon - soap
habubo - impetuous
habune - to lather, soap up
hacha - to tenderize
hachaigua - similar
hachita - hatchet
hado - godson
hae - brow, forehead

hafa - what, matter
hafa taimano - in what manner
hafe - splint, splinter
hafno' - high tide
hafot - to bury, entomb
haga - blood, daughter
hagahaf - sand crab (black type)
hagas - in old times
haggan - turtle
hagoi - pond
hagoñg - to breathe
haguha - asthmatic, needle
haguhi - sand crab
haha - to blow, breathe
hahanon - burning
i hahatme guma/ sake' - burglar
haiguas - coconut shell
hailas - poverty, want
hakmang, titohge - moray eels
hala - to pull, haul
halacha - sometime ago, past
halak - scarcehalañg - to terrify
hale' - let's go! (animals)
halige' - pole, stake
halion - eradicable
halom - inside, within
halom tano' - jungle
haluman - to lose one's life
halu'o - shark
ham - us
hamafak - brittle, fragile
hamaleffa - forgetful
hamañiente - irritable, touchy
hamas - ever
hambriento - greedy, gluttonous
hame - to warm
hamlañgo - sickly
hamon - ham
hamyo - you (plural)
hanague - to go through
hanao - to go, leave
hanaotati/debuetta - backwards
hanhan - to threaten with gestures

hanom - water
hanom inestila - distilled water
hanon - to burn up
hañgai - to want to
hao - you
ha'of - chest
hara - water pitcher, jug
harina - flour
hasan - rare, unusual, famine
hasayaihon - to bear in mind
hasienda - farm, residence, possessions
hasngon - intentional, premeditated
hasngot - ginger
haspok - full
hasso - to think, reflect
hasta - flag mast, until
hasta ñgai'an? - until when?
hasuli - eel
hasulon - slippery
hasusuye - intending
hasuye - to estimate, calculate
hasuye demasiao - to worry too much, brood
hatalapos - destitute, worn, ragged
hatdin - garden
hatdinero - gardener
hatme - to go in, enter
hatpon - harpoon
hatsa - to lift, ascend, advance, promote
hatsamiento - rebellion, mutiny
hatutungoha - knowingly
hatungo umatte - artful
hauhau - sound of a dog barking (i.e. woof-woof, arf-arf)
haye - who? which?
hayeha - whoever
hayo - wood, timber
hayon matutong - fuel (for cooking, fire)
hebiyas - buckle
hechura - characteristic, feature
hechuran taotao - humanity
hedo - to dry up, shrivel, tuck in (clothes)
hefe - chief
helengga - syringe
hemplo - legend

henerasion - generation
henero - January
henguan - probable
henio - mood, mind
henngan - mob, unruly crowd
hentan - to find, meet
heografia - geography
heometria - geometry
heramienta - tool
heramienta para man aprieta - clamp
hereda - to inherit
heredero - heir
herehe - heretic
herensia - inheritance
hereria - smith
herero - blacksmith
heresia - heresy
herida - wound
hetbana - to patch together
hichom - shutters
higado - liver
higante - giant (person)
higef - to surprise, catch unaware
higera - fig tree
higos - fig
hihihot/adbiento - advent
hihokok - fleeting, perishable
hihoroba - annoying
hihosguan - distrustful person
hihot - adjacent, concise, near
hikamas - sweet turnip
hila - to spin
hilera - row of houses
hilo - thread
i hilo ogso - top of a hill, mountain peak
hiloña - over, above, near
hima - trident
hinafa - object, thing
hinafno i tasi - incoming tide
hinagong - breath
hinagong na fehman - to breathe hard
hinalom - the inner soul, entrance, mental (psyche)
hinanao - departure

hinasgune - malice
hinasso - memory, reason, understanding
hinasson atmariao - delerium
hinatme - invasion
hinatme manglo - flatulence
hineka - harvest
hineksa' - cooked rice
hinemeninatan - eyesore
hinemhom - darkness
hinemlo – health, recovery
hineroba – annoyance
hiniga – strong wind
hinigef – ambush
hinilat – power, strength
hinilat maisa – self-control
hiniyong – effect, consequence
hipato – pale, light
hipokresia – hypocrisy
hipokrito/ kado mamamaulek –hypocrite
hysteria – hysteria
hit – us
hita – wehoben – young
hoflak – to lick
hogadot – gambler
hogue – to carry a child
hogete' – toy
hohomhom – twilight
hohosguan - envious
hoka – to pluck, pick
hokok – ruined, lost
hokok ñalang – starvation
home – to darken, overshadow
homhom – obscure, dark
homlo – to revive, recover from illness
homlo ta'lo - revival
honesto - honest, honorable
hongang – to amaze, scare
hongge – to believe, devout
hongguiyon – by chance, credible
honra - to honor
hoño – to crush
hotka – gallows, execute
hotkon – pillar

hotge – to befall, happen
hotma – to build
hotnalero – day worker
hotne – to pierce
hotno – oven
hotyat – to scratch off
hoyo – excavation
hubentud - youth
huchom – to enclose
huchom duro – to slam (loud)
huebes – Thursday
huego – game
huegon salape – to gamble
huerfana/o - orphan
hues – judge
hugando – to play
hugahnom – to dissolve, melt
hugum – to oppress
huho – to bid
huisio – sentence (law)
hula – tongue
hulat – to overcome, conquer
hule – oilcloth
hulo –thunder
hulok – to snap, break
hulos – to smooth out
I humahalom – income from labor
humalom – to suppose
humanao – to proceed
humanao para otro tano – to emigrate
humanaohulo – upward
humekua – doubtful
humihot – to approach
humuyongña – to result in
huna – poison, poisonous
hunggan – yes
hungok – to hear, listen
hunta – assembly
hunto – fat
husga – to award
husto – just, impartial
hutu – to use up, weed out
huyong – get outside, out!

i - the
i'e' - infant jacks (fish)
iba' - a type of sour fruit that resebmles grapes
ibidensa - proof, facts
idea - idea
identifika - to identify
idioma - idiom, certain characteristic of a language
idolo - idol
i'esitan - joker, jester
igi - defeat, beat
ignoransia - ignorance
ignorante - ignorant
igu - jealousy
i'isao - sinner
ikak - to defeat (competition)
ilek - said
ilotes - corn on the cob
imbentibu - inventive, creative
impetuosu - impetuous, passionate, irritable
impide - to restrain
impolitiko - impolite
impone - to lay on, impose
imposipble - impossible
impotta - import
impottante - important
imprenta/impresot - printer
impresa - to impress
imprudensia - carelessness
impuesto - delivery, draft, excise, duty
in - we
ina - to light up
inabak - error, misunderstanding
inabmam - to stop, delay
inabundansia - superfluous
inachago - distance
inachatli'e - hatred
inadayao - to become interested
inafliton batatas - potato chips
ina'gang - noise, loudness
inakacha - deception, to do damage
inakka - to sting
inarekkla - method or system

inatditi - oppressed, worsened
infelis - unhappy
infietno - hell
ingratu - ungrateful
inhuria - to revile
iniga - to caress
inigo' - jealousy
inklinao - inclination towards something
inkombinensia - inconvenience
imottat - immortal
insima - to intensify
insutta - to insult
intelihente - intelligent
interesao - selfish (also chattao)
inturompe - to interrupt
introdusi - introduce
inutet - paralyzed, unserviceable
ipe' - cut open, chip
ira - catastrophe
isa - rainbow
isao - sin
isla - island
isleta - small island
Istoria Sagrada - Biblical history
iya' – by the way (term used to start a new sentence)
iyo - belong to

Julio - July
Junio - June

kadada' - short
kafe - coffee
kahet - orange
kahet ma'gas - grapefruit
kakaguates - peanuts
kalakas - disgusting
kalaktos - sharp
kalan - like, as
ka'lanke - little finger
kalessa - carriage
ka'lulot - fingers
ka'lulot talo' - middle
kamisola - slip

kamuti - sweet potatoes
kannai - arm, hand
kantit - cliff
kanton tasi - beach
karabao - carabao
kareta - car, vehicles on wheels
karetan guaka - bullcart
karetan hayu - bullcart
karetan kahon - boxcart wagon
karetan trosu - bullcart
karetiya - wagon
katadu - spoiled milk
katne - meat
katnen babui - pork
katnen binadu - deer meat
katnen chiba - goat meat
katnen guaka - beef
katnen karabao - carabao meat
katnen notte - whole corned beef
kato - cat
katsunes - pants
ketu! - keep still!
kichu - convict
kilu'os tasi - starfish
kiridu/a - sweetheart
kitan - cross-eyed
klase - class, type
krakas - crackers
kunehu - rabbit

la'abmam - for quite some time
laba - to nail, fasten
labadot - lavatory
labios - lips
labit - violin
labla - to carve (wood, stone, etc.)
lacha - to lay in mud
lachai - to consume, leaving nothing
lache - wrong, faulty, injustice
ladera - cliff
ladriyo - brick, tile
ladron - thief
laet - to hurt, grieve

lago - melted, tear
laguana - soursop
lagua - net
laguaña - soursop tree
lahi - male
lahyan - many
lai - law
lakse - to sew, stitch
laktus - thorn, thistle
lala - vivacious, robust
lalache an kumentos - to stammer in speech
lalalaha - to survive, outlive, outlast
lalanghita - tangerine
lalango - fainting
lalangoñaihon - faint
lalatde ta'lo - to object, oppose
lalat-diyon - culpable, needing censure
lalo - fly
lamagong - to recuperate, lessen in severity
lamas - to rot
lamasa - table
lamen - to wound, beat
lamentasion - lamentation, moan, wail
lamita - half
lamlam - bright, pure, shining
lamlam mahlos - polished
lamok - to stink
lampasu - mop, cleaning rag
lana - wool
lanan - to snore
lanchita - yacht
lancho - ranch, farm
laña - interjection, i.e. wow! damn! what?! etc.
langa - someone who's easily tricked, simpleton
langhet - sky, heaven
laniya - flannel
lansa - lance
lanseta - lancet
lao - side
lapida - tombstone
lapis - pencil
largeru - shaft (vehicle)
lasa - to rub, massage

lasarino - leprosy
lasas - skin, outer shell, husk
lasas atadok - eyelid
laso - lasso
lastre - ballast
lata - can
late' - scab, itch
latigaso - to chastise with a rod, switch
latfena - foward!
latga - envious, jealous or stingy
latga bista - spyglass
latgero - pole
latigo - whip
lato - slippery
laton - brass
lau - but, nevertheless
laulau - tremble, shake
laulau ma'añao - to tremble with fear, terror
lauya - kettle
layak - sail
layau - to stroll around
layo -to envy
leba i ankla - anchor
lebadura - yeast
lebbok - murky
legat - legal
legitimo - legitimate
legua - league, mile
lehngon - shady
lektura - lecture
lelikui - to surround, encompass
lemenda - to mend
lemlemtaotao/tigefhomhom - melancholy, gloom, obscurity
lemmai - breadfruit
lemmon adamelong - lemon lime type
lemmon china - southeast asian lemon
lemmon riat - a common type of lemon
lemonada - lemonade
lemunayas - illumination
lente - lens
leon - lion
lepblo - book
lepblon kuenta - account book, ledger

leston - edge, ledge
letania - litany
letke - to evade, flee
letran atfabeto - letter of the alphabet
leyok - hollow
libettad - liberty, freedom
libra - pound
libre - free, safe
licheng - fishing tackle
lichera - dairy
li'i - to see, look, glance, perceive
li'ion - visible
likot - liquor
liliko - bent, curved, crooked
lima - to file, a file
limite - to restrict, limit
limon - acid lime
limosna - alm
linabla - a carving
linache - fiasco, failure, error
linailes - wiles
linahyan - party
linala - life, evolution, existence
linala i tataotao ta'lo - resurrection
linamlam - radiance, luster
linamon - skill
linao - earthquake
linatga - avarice
linea - line
lineat - lineal (ancestry)
lineka - height
lini'i - vision
linihan - panic
lini'i i atadok - eyesight, line of sight
linimiento - liquid, topical medication
linimutan - moldy
linipa - cheating, deceit
lino - linen
li'of - to dive
lipa - to conceal
lirio - lily
lisayo - rosary
lisensia - license

liso - sleek
lista - list
listo - quick-witted, smart, prepared
literat - literal
liti - to mix, thin
litrato - picture, photo
liyang - cave
lodo - obese
logra - to conquer, acquire
lokat - local
lokka' - tall
lokkue' - also, too
loklok - to boil, cook
loko - crazy
lo'lo - cough
lolosos - rattle in the throat
lomo - hip, groin area
lona - canvas
lonnat - birthmark
losa - stone slab
losus - hoarse
loteria - raffle, lottery
lotge - to fill, pour
lotgun - to fall in a pit, hole
lucha - row
lucho - acute
luga - wall
lugat - place
luhan/Lujan - worried
luhurioso - luxurious
lukau - procession
lulai - fishing during moonlight
lulok – nail (also: lulok hao - enjoy yourself)
luluhan - anxious
luluke - to nail down
lumagas - to slide
luma'la - to be, exist
luma'la guaha - to propser
lumalalo - to ferment
lumamagof - to relieve/free from pain, grief
lumamaulek - to improve, advance, progress
lumamagai - to enlarge, increase
luma'ong - to loaf around

lumatailaye - to get worse
luma'uya - to wander about, to idle
lumayak - to sail
lumos - to merge, absorb, swallow
lumot - moss
lumus - to immerse
lumut - a type of seaweed
lunes - Monday
luño - sandy
lupis - skirt (clothing)
lus elektisida - electricity/light
lusong - mortar
luto - mourning, grief, sorrow
ma'agsom - sour, acidic, tart
ma'añao - afraid, timid
ma'ase - compassionate, merciful, forgiveness
ma'asen - fogiveness
ma'ataska - to be caked with mud
ma'ayek - preferred
mabira - turn
mabotda - embroidery
machachalane - instructed
machalehgua - diffused
machakchak katan - dawn
machalupun - scattered
machalek - coarse, stubborn, fierce
machat atan - hated, odious, hateful
maches - matches
machete - bush knife
macheten matadot - meat cleaver
maching - monkey, ape
machocho duro - hard labor
machom - closed
madefiefiende - client (of a lawyer)
madeha - piece of thread
maderas - building material
madesokupa - desolate, uninhabited
madestrosa - to devastate, ruined
madirihe - guidance, direction
madok - cavity
madok atgoya - harness for carabao (ring in nose)
madok tataotao - skin pores
madulalak - expulsion, ejection

maenbatsama - to embalm
maestro - teacher, boss
maetdot - numb, no sensation
mafaborerese - the favorite child
mafak - wreck
mafakai - partition
mafak atagtagña - pacified
mafahiyong - to despise, slander
mafamaolek - to rally, collect
mafamaolek i nilache - to right a wrong
mafañago - to be born
mafañago i mismo tano - indigenous
mafnot - sturdy, robust
mafondo - to sink, sunk
mafti - knife blade notch
mafunas - to exterminate, annihilate
mafuti - a type of fish, snapper
maga - early
magagu - clothes
magahan - green-blue parrotfish
magahit - certain, sure
magalahi - magistrate, governor
magaom hinalom - grateful, sympathetic
magao - to yawn
magas - grand, exalted
magas i batko - sea captain
magas na isao - capital sin
magase - to rule, dominate
magefatan - liked
mageftungo - popular, well-liked by others
magem - moist or silent
magguag - roomy
magi - here, this way
magmata - to wake up
magnganite - Satan
magof - happy
magofli'e - beloved
magpo - to finish, be ready
mahaga - to bleed
mahalang - painful, sorrow, to yearn
mahalangue - to grieve
mahangue - stale, rancid
mahañas - soft

mahedo - to shrink, wrinkle
mahetok - hardened in feelings, firm, strong
mahetok ni manengheng - frozen
mahgef/yayas - tired
mahimahi - dolphinfish
mahlok - bone fracture
mahlos - smooth, level
mahanau - to return
mahngang - stunned
maho - thirsty
mahongang - lobster
mahuto - roomy
maigo - sleep
maigo ñaihon - to snooze, sleep lightly
maila - to come
ma'is - corn
maipe - hot
mairasta - stepmother
maisa - self, one's self, only
makalamya - handy, nimble, agile
makalehlo - wrinkle
makamu - wedding ceremony (at the altar)
makansela - to cancel
makana - to hang
makaro' - yellowfin (fish)
makaron - macaroni
makat - heavy
makolat - siege
makone - captured
makonsagra - consecration
maktan - gutter, canal
makuaha - curdled milk
makulatum - rough
makupa - mountain apple
malachai - completely used up
malaet - sour
malago - to want
malago na u sangan - to insinuate, imply
malagon taotao - fugitive
malagredesido - ungrateful
malak - went to
malamaña - uncivil, rough, savage
malango - sick, ill

malasas - bruise
malate' - learned, sharp, intelligent
malayo - dry, wilted
malefa - to forget
mal ehemplo - bad example
maleta - suitcase
mali'i - appearance, vision
malinao - calm
malingo - deprivation, loss, take away, gone
mal intensionao - evil-minded
malisia - malice
malofan - to pass by
malulok - free, undisturbed
malumorado - bad-humor
malumut - sickening smell, contagious
mama - drinkable
mama' - to play dead
ma'ma - to chew
mamababas - cheating, swindling
mamabehiga - blister
mamacha - sense of touch
mamagasiyan - wash basin
mamahlao - to be ashamed
mamaichecho - to struggle, scuffle
mamaigo - sleeper
mamaisa - solitary
mamakano - edible
mamalahi - manly, courageous
mamama'gas - stuck-up, opinionated
i mamamaila - the future
mamamaila na tiempo - in the future
mamamaneska - to brew, make liquor
mamamta - fruitful, fertile
mamanunui - pioneer
mamatago - inferior, subordinate
mamatai - mortal
mamatatati - to hesitate, linger, be late, slow
mamatate - to straggle, lag
i mamatinas planon guma - architect
mamatkilo - silent, tranquil
mamatki'kilo - calm, tranquil
mamaudai - rider
mamaya - navigable, superficial

i mamemedos - climber
mamehora - to improve
mames - sweet
mamfok - to weave
mamokat - to walk
mampos - unnecessary, too much of s.t.
mamuda - dolled-up
mamulan - skipjack fish (large)
i mamumulan - a guard
mamuno - to murder
mamuten tataotao - rheumatism
maña - trick
mana daña - mixed up
manada - herd
manadahe - to hoard, collect
ma na kalamtenña - transfer, removal
man adanche - symmetrical
manadidide i minegae - summary of contents
i man adodora idolo - idolatry
manahuyung - creation, work, piece
manakihom - frugal, thrifty
manakilisayon - to baptize, christen
manamtam - joy, taste
ma na nuebuña - renewal, renovation
manapayon - habitual, customary
man aregla - ruler (person)
ma na santos - sacred
man atma - stubborn
man burukuento - noisy (crowd)
manbula - swollen
mancha - blemish, stain
manda - imperative, obligatory
mandagi - deceit
man despetdisia - to pillage
man dibe - to be in debt
manea - business transaction, negotiation or behave
i man ekunguk - listeners
maneha - to use, manage
manempeya - greasy, fatty
manengheng - cold, chilly
manesgue - to steal
man espia - to do/perform a reconnaisance
man eyak - instructed

manflores - to blossom
mangag - to stagger, sag, bend down
mangentataye - seller
mangfong - to reckon
mangga - mango
manggas - sleeve
mangge - where
mangi - delicious
mangko - one-armed
mangle - mangrove
manglo' - wind, air
mango - saffron (used in Spanish cooking)
mangofli'e - benevolent
i manguaiya - sweetheart
i manguiguifi - a dreamer
manha - tender coconut
man hale - to take root
man hasso - to recollect
manhongge - vituous
manhufa - to stretch out both arms
manhufa para u - to pledge allegiance to
manhulat - powerful
manhulon - noble
manhungok - hearing
i manlili'e - spectator
manman - wondering, dazed
manmerese - deserving, worthy
mannok - chicken
manohu - a bundle
manokcha - to bear fruit, sprout
mansanan agaga' - red apple
mansanan betde - green apple
mansangan - rumor has it, current story
mansanita - panama cherry
manso - gentle, refined
manteles - table or altar cloth
mantension - livelihood
mantiene - help, aid, grasp
mantika - lard, fat
mantikan leche - heavy cream/milk
mantikiya - butter
manu - where
manufaktura - to manufacture

manugong - to bolt a door
manungo - scholar
man yuyute - to ravage
mañagi - to loot
mañahak - anchovies
mañahalom gi lista - to enlist, enroll
mañaina - ancestors
i mañangangane - an informer
mañaña - smooth, glossy
mañetnot - evil, diseased
mañgagmona - to bend down and forward
mañila - flame, fire
mañila ensigidas - sudden flash of light
mañiñila - glistening, shining
mañom - head cold, congestion
mañotsot - to reform
mañugo - to fester, rot
mañuso - to grow back (plants)
maolek - good
mapa - map
mapagahes - cloud
mapanas - flat, level, stone
masoksok - skinny
matanhanom - waterfall
ma'te' - low tide
Matso - March
mattingan - reef
maug - stronge, lasting
Mayu - May
melokoton - peaches
melon - cantelope
mendioka - tapioca
meyas - socks
minnes - mannowfish
motosaikot - motorcycle
mumu - fight
muta - vomit
mutung - foul smelling, stink

na - that, the, which
na'abmam - to postpone
na'adingo - to sequester
na'adispatta - to disassemble

na'adotgan - to pierce through
na'afamaolek - to atone
na'agadon - to confuse
na'agaoli - to cross one's legs
na'ahustao - to adjust
na'ali - to insult
na'alibiao - to alleviate
na'an - name
na'ancho - to widen
na'animoso - to make stronger
na'anok - to discover
na'apaka - to whitewash
na'apaling - to wring out (as in a dishrag)
na'apo - to hold back
na'asegura - to assert
na'asentado - to accomodate
na'asgon - to soil
na'atarantao - to disunite
na'atborotao - troublesome
na'attilong - to blacken
na'atok - to conceal
na'atulaika - to barter or trade
na'aya - to forge, make equal
na'ayao - to borrow
nabaha - pocketknife, razorblade
nabegadot - navigator
nabelembao - to vibrate, to shake something
nabeste - to adorn
nabio - navy
naboka - to feed
nabrabo - to strengthen, enliven
nabubo - to provoke, make angry
nabubu - insolent
nabula - to fill up
nachaka - to snap, break
nachaddek - to hustle
nachalek - amusing, funny
nachaochao - to fluctuate
nachatguiya - despiser
nachathagong - to suffocate
nachathinasso - to embarrass
nachatpago - to deface, disfigure
nachatsaga - to annoy, outrage

nachaoli i dadalak - to wag the tail
nachetan - to strain, stretch
nacheton - to connect, stick
nachilong - to arrange proportionally
nadangkolo mas ke i minagahet - to exaggerate
nadaña - to mingle, mix
nadenga - to turn upside down
nadespresiao - to bring into contempt
nadilok - to reverse
nadinanche - to rectify, set right
nadogae - to confound, tire
na'empas - to give satisfaction
na'entalo - to shove in
na'esponha - to inflate, swell
na'etnon - to gather, pluck
na'eyak - to educate
nafache - to smear
nafailek - bitter, acidic
nafakpo - to enter an agreement
nafalingo - to destroy
nafalofan - to let come to pass
nafamta - to bring forth
nafamatkilo - to appease
nafana'an - to dominate
nafanagitilu'i - to pile up
nafañetnot - to wound
nafañila - to ignite, turn on
nafañotsot - to reform
nafanungo - to illuminate
nafanyaoyao - to instigate
na'i - to give
na'i grasias - to thank
na'i notisia - to give notice
na'i pasto - to graze
na'i patte - to communicate, share
na'i petmiso - to agree to, give permission
na'i prenda - to be responsible
nakabales - to perfect
nakachang - to dirty, diminish
nakadada - to abridge
nakafache - to soil with mud
nakahulo - to raise up
nakalaktus - to sharpen

nakalamten - to set in motion
nakalo - to slacken
nakaloha - to provoke
nakapkap - to make room
nakayada - to mitigate
naklaruye - to explain, interpret
nanu - midget
napu - wave
natata - shallow
nateng - slow
ngosngos - squid
nifen - teeth
nika - sweet yam
niyok - coconut

-ña - his, her
ña - more, better
ñaba - pliable
ñahlalang - lightweight
ñahlalang na minaigo - to sleep lightly
ñaihon - awhile
ñaka - to hang up, suspend
ñalang - hungry
ñama - helpless
ñamu - mosquito
ñangnang - arrogant, entertaining, talkative
ñango - hips
ñangon - to whisper secretively
ñangu - swim
ñaño - dull
ñating - slow
ñauhan - to stagger
ñehong - to duck, humble one's self
-ñiha - their, theirs
ñinalang - hunger
ñiñiña - to caress or a flatterer
ñogñog - to submerge in water
ñohmon - wet (muddy)
ñoño - to merge, swallow up
ñudo - to button
ñukot - to strangle
ñumangu - swam
ñuña - to fondle, pet

obehas - sheep
obispo - bishop
obliga - to imply or impose
obligao - compulsory
obligasion - obligation
obra na karidat - work of love
obtuso/taipunta/foda - obtuse, dull
ochenta - eighty
ocho - eight
odda' - dirty
odda' fache - dirt, dung
odda yan mititek - shabby, mean-looking
odio - hatred, spite
ofaisen - to seek information
ofende - offend
ofisiat - official
ofisina/ofisio - office
ofresi/kombida - bid, offer
ogan - to go ashore, run aground, strand
ogga'an - morning
ogso - mountain
ohalatero - plumber
ohales - buttonhole
ohas - leaf
okasion - occasion
okodo - sling, trap, ruse
okodon chaka - rat trap
oksidente - the Occident, the West
okso' - hill
Oktobre - October
okupa - to occupy
okupante - occupant
okupasion - calling, vocation
o'mak - swim, bathe
o'mak riegadera - (n.) shower
omlat - to contain, hold within
onginge' - to get a scent
onse - eleven
opagat - crosswise, in opposition to
opan - echo
operasion - operation
opio - opium

opone - to contradict, disagree
opopone - resisting
oposision - opposition
opottunidat - opportunity
opottuno/kontiempo - opportune, well-timed
oppe - reply, answer
oppop - lie down on stomach
oprime - to oppress, stifle, subdue
ora - time, hour
oras - hours
oriente - Orient
oriya - border, end, limit
oriyan - beside, in proximity
oriyan tasi - the coast, shoreline
oriyaye - to encompass
oro - gold
osgon - dutiful, obedient
osgi - to listen to, obey
osila - to oscillate, swing back and forth
osiosiadat - idleness
osioso - leisure
oso - bear
o'son - tired, weary, bored
ospitat - hospital
otadnon - to ramble, wander
otden - command, order
otdena - to decree, direct, ordain
otdinario - customary, ordinary
otdinario na taotao - common people
otdon - prickly heat
otdot - ant
otguyoso - proud
otkesta - orchestra
otobai' - motorcycle
otra manera - otherwise
otro - other, else
otro na simana - next week
ottografia - orthography

pabu - turkey
pacha - to touch
pachakate - small (growth)
pachang - tender

pachot - mouth
pachuchang - neat, gorgeous
pada - to box or slap someone
padadag - deceit, denial
padadang - drooping pants/rear end
padit - wall
padrigiyos - to chain or fetter
pagadot - paymaster
pagano - pagan
pagat - to advise or counsel
pagngas - to cut, split
pago - now, today
pago finañago - infancy, early childhood
pa'gogoha - actual
pago manana - daybreak, twilight, dawn
pago yan ayo - now and then
pagpag - blister; to smack with tongue
paha - straw, stalk
paharon u oriyan tasi - gull, sea-gull
pahgang - clam
pahon - screw pine, used for weaving
paine - comb
painen basula - rake
pairasto - stepfather
pais - region
pakaka! - hush!
pakyo - typhoon
pala - shovel, spade
palabra ni honrao - word of honor
palacha - swindler
paladat - palate, roof of mouth
paladan - scar, wound, wheal
palai - oitment for wounds
palaga - to slip
palakse - smooth, slippery
palangana - pan, frying pan or washbasin
palagpang - roar, cry, or loud noise
palapa - to flutter or flap wings
palaspas - to splash; to do something superficially; to dabble
palasyo - palace
palao'an, hembra - female, woman
pale - father, priest
Palestina, Tierra Santa - Holy Land, Palestine

paleta - painter's palette
palo - some, more or less, partly, stake
palon batko - mast of ship
paluma - bird
pake - rifle, gun
paken petdegon - shotgun
pakete - parcel, small bundle
pan - bread
panadero - baker
panak - to strike
panak-lalo' - fly swatter
panak tenis - tennis racket
pañales - mantilla (Spanish garment)
panglao - crab
panglao oru - golden sea crab
pangon, yaho - to arouse, wake up
pañite - to strike, shit
paño - handkerchief, kerchief
pañot ales - to gulp down without chewing
pantalan - pier, wharf
pantaya, homen kandet - screen or lampshade
pañuelon - shawl, shoulder wrap
Papa, i Santo Papa - the Pope, the Holy Father
papa - papal, pertaining to the Roman Catholic Church
papa - wing or underneath
papacha - pathetic, touching
papakyo - stormy
papalote - kite; dragon
papakes - nails (fingers, toes)
papakes ga'ga' - hoof (animals)
papatte - parting or separating
papau - a plant that grows along streams
papaya - papaya
papeleta, sedula - ticket
papet -paper
papet asero - sandpaper
para - for, in place of
para - to stop
parada - parade, military display
paraiso - chinaberry
parafo - clause
paralitico - paralysis, palsy
para ma na lago - for broiling, beef for broiling

para man remotke - tug, tugboat
para mona - henceforth, in the future
parannaihon - attitude, position
para papa - downward, toward the ground
para todo - universal, general, for all
para u siña - to enable, to make able
parejo - alike, resembling, similar, simultaneous, kindred
parentesis - parenthesis
parereho - oppressive
pares - pair
parientes - relatives
paroko - curate of a parish
parokia - parish
pas - peace
pasadero - transient
pasadot - razor sharpener
pasahe - passage through, transit
pasahero - passenger, traveler
paska - fragile
Pasgua - Easter
pasifiko -peaceful
pasion - passion
paso - pace, setp, manner of walking
pastet - pie
pasto - pasture, to graze, meadow
pastot - herder, shepherd
pat -either, or
patang - shield
patas - foot, sole
patas ga'ga' - paw
patek - to wince, shrink
patgon - child
patgon kabayo - colt
patgon chiba - kid (young goat)
patgon na trongko - sapling, young tree
patio - yard, courtyard
patlino - godfather
patma - palm (hand); palm tree
patmada - to slap with an open hand
patol - abdomen, groin
patke - park
patriatka - patriarch
patriotiko - patriotism

patron - patron, protector
patron galaide - steersman
patruya - patrol (police)
patte - part, share, partial
patte gi tataotao - body part
pattikulat - particular, excellent
pattida - ration, departure
pattidon - party
patto - midwife
pau - scent, odor, aroma, savor, sense of smell
paupau - fragrant
pausa - pause
pausado - leisurely
payaya - frigate bird
payo - parasol,unmrella
payon - skilled, experienced, to become accustomed
pechau - to run away, jump
pecho - chest
pedasito - slice, scrap, thin piece, atom, particle
pedaso - block of wood, stone
pedason magagu ni dalalai - tape, narrow band of cloth
pedason tano - region of a country
pega - to set, place in position, to stick
peka - office
pekado beniat - venial sin
pekadot - sinner
pekno - murderous, cruel
peligro - danger, peril
peligroso - dangerous, risky
peludo - hairy, wooly
pena de muette - death penalty
peniti - full of grief
penitensia - penance, atonement
penitiyiye - sympathizing, grateful
pennga, kostumbre - custom
pension - pension
penta - to draw, sketch
peon - day laborer
pepega' - cone shell
pepino - cucumber
pepitas - seed, kernel
peras - pear
periodo - period, span of time

perito - expert
pes - pitch
pesa, minakat - to weigh, weight
pesadot - scale, balance
pesadumbre - anger, vexation
peskadot, talayero - fisherman
peson - to pound, ram
pespes - to rustle, to murmur
peste - pestilence, plague
petbetso - infamous, wicked
petde - to overcome, subdue
petdon - forgiveness, pardon
petfekto - ideal, perfect
pethudika, inakacha - to impair, prejudice, to do damage
pethuisio - harm, loss, to lose
petlas - pearl
petmanente - permanent
petmite - to permit, to consent
petrolio - petroleum
petsan - to rebound, to recoil
petsige - to persecute or pursue
petsona - person
pettenese - to pertain to
piano - piano
pi'ao - reed, bamboo
pi'ao lahi - thorny type of bamboo
pi'ao palao'an - smooth type of bamboo
piesa - piece of cloth
pietna - bone, leg
piga - giant taro
pika - spicy or sharp
pikaro - pervert, man without honor, villain
pikatdia - roguery
piknik - picnic
piko - spout, beak
pi'ot - sour plum
pikols - cucumber
piloto - pilot
piloton aire - aviator
pilotuye - to pilot
pimienta - pepper
piña - pineapple
pinadesi - grievance, a sense of wrong, agony

pinagat - counsel, advice
pinalakse - fluent in speech
pinalala - to hurry, to be hasty
pinalalala - scrupulous
pinañot - gulp, dram
pinareho - identical, likeness
pinarehon i dos raya punta a punta - parallel
pinatgon - infancy, early childhood
pinaupau - spice
pinayon - dexterity
pineble - poverty, penury
pinekat - walk
pineksai - propagation
pinelo - stock, store
pinengle - restriction
pinenta - draft, sketch, painting
pinetsige' - persecution
pinigan - glow of burning coals, charcoal
pinine - refusal, rejection
pinino maisa - suicide
pinite - grief, sorrow
pinitiye - to grieve, lament
pino - pine tree
pinto - free will, caprice
pintura - paint, enamel
pipa - barrel
i pipenta - painter
pipinu - a type of watermelon: small, yellow
pipupu - type of fish
pirata - pirate
pisara - slate
piso - floor
pistola - pistol
pitdora - pill, medicine
plaito - to litigate, contest in a court of law
plaiton familia - feud
plalanta - founder, builder
planas - plains
plancha - picture
planchansin - corrugated iron
planeta - planet
plano - plan
planta - to institute, till the fields

planta i lamasa - set the table
plantasma - spook, a certain type of ghost
plantet - nursery
plasa - plaza
plaso - respite, term, fixed term
plata - silver
platea - silver
platero - silversmith
plato - dish, platter
platon fonografo - phonographic record
pliego - sheet of paper
plomiso - made of lead
plomo - lead
pluma - feather
plumahe - plumage
poblasion - population
poble - poor
podlilo - spoiled, offensive, foul
podong - to tumble or fall
podonghalom - to collapse, break down
poesia - poetry
pokat - to step, tread
pokat taiguihi i pokat kabayo - trot
pokpok - sore, ulcer
poksai - to fatten
poksen - to spoil, to become foul in odor
politiko - polite; political
po'lo - to put; to permit
polonñaihon - to interrupt, hold up
polonon - black filefish
ponedera - brood hen
pongle - to imprison
ponson - bodkin
pontan - fallen coconut
popa - stern of a ship
popodong -falling, sinking
posible - possible
posision - position
positibo - positive
poso - well
postiso - support, platform
postre - dessert
pot - because

potahe - mush, broth
potbola - powder
potbolan pake - gunpowder
potbos - fog
potbos katbon - coal dust
pot enao - thus, so then
pot espasio de - while, during the time that
potfia - to molest
potfiao - inflexible, rigid
pot fin - finally
pot i fuetsa - forcible, violent
potga - cathartic medicine
potgas - flea
poto - rice cake
potpot - thick, wide
potpot labiosña - thick-lipped
potkeria - trifle
pot sea akaso, yanggin - in case
potso - shrewd; marksman
potta - door
pottamoneda - purse
poyo - young rooster
poyon duendes - sponge, mushroom
praktiko, esperimentao - usage
prenda - sign, mark, token
prensa - iron
prensa para fugo laña o asaite - wine press, oil press
prensipiante, aprendis - novice, beginner
prepara - to prepare
preparye - to equip
presa - river dam; stem; resist
presensia - attendance
presio - price, to prize
presion aminudo - retail price
presision - precision
presiso - certain
preso - to capture, take prisoner
presomido - ill-natured, rough
presta - to lend
prestada - loan
pribilegio - privilege
primabera - spring
primerisa - first birth

primet biahe - to use for the first time
primo - cousin
prinemete - promise, vow
prinepara - preparation
prinsipat - principal; capital; important
prinsipatmente - mainly
prinsipio - start
prision - prison
prisionero - prisoner
probecho - advantage, gain, yield
probechoso - useful, lucrative
probinsia - to supply with food
probision nengkanno - food ration
problema - problem
probokatibo - provoking
prokura - to procure
prodigo - spendthrift, gallant
produktoso - fruitful
profana - profane
profeta - prophet
prohibe - to prohibit
promesa - security, pledge
promete - to promise
pronunsia - to pronounce
propiedat tano - real estate
propietario - landlord
propio, umaya - becoming, proper
propone - to propose
proposision - proposition
propatsion - proportion
protektot - guardian, protector
protehe - to protect
protesta - to protest
prueba - to verify; evidence, testimony
pruibido - forbidden
publika - to divulge, publish
publikao - notoriety, publicly known
publiko - general, public
puenge - night
puetka - female pig
puetto - port
puetton seguro - safe haven
pugas - uncooked rice

pugua - betel but
puge - to feed
pugi - to decoy, allure into danger
puha - to overthrow; loam
puhot - to oppress
pula - to explain, solve
pulan - moon, month; keep watch
pulaon - soluble
pulatat - water hen
pulido - polished
pulo - hair, pubic hair
pulon ga'ga' - animal fur
pulon mannok - feathers
pulon tengho - mane
pumalalapa - a flap
pumara - pause
pumarannaihon - tp loiter or linger, to hesitate
pumareho - equivalent
pumayaya - adrift
puminite - to regret, rue
pumokpok - inflating, swelling
pune - to recant or deny
punen maisa - self-control, self-denial
puno' - turn off/kill
puno' maisa - to commit suicide
punta - point
puntan achai - point of the chin
puntan hasta - top of the mast
puntan osgo - top of a mountain
puntat - bracket
puntero - stick, pointer
puntuat -punctual
pupuenge - evening
puro - merely, simply
puta - whore
puten chachak - colic
putgada - inch
puti - pain
puti'on - star
putlilo - to rot or spoil
putpito - pulpit
putseras - bracelet
putso - pulse

rabanos - radish
rabia - rage
rai – king
raina – queen
rainado - reign
raino - kingdom
ramas - twig, branch
ramiyete - bouquet
ramo - rank, position
rana, kairo - frog
rasa - race, breed
rasguno - tear, fissure
rasimo - bunch
rason - statement, reason
rasonapble - reasonable
raspa - to scrape or rub off
rastrea - to track or search out
rastro - scent, sense of smell
rato - moment
raya - line, length
reatmente - really
rebaha - to lower the price
reberensia - to revere, pay homage
rebetde - stubborn
rebista - to review, correct
rebolusion - revolution
rebotbida - to reverberate
rebotsion - revulsion (sudden)
rebuetbe - to revoke, dismiss
rebuetbe - revolver (gun)
rechachasa - resisting
rechasa - to resist
redima - redemption
redito - revenue
rediu - radio
refiere - to refer, sumbit
refleho - to reflect
refotma - to reform
refreresko - refreshing
refresko - to refresh
regalo - gift
regla - order, command, or ruler

regula - to regulate
regulat - regular
regulatmente - regularly
rehas - rail, bar, lattice
rehimiento - regiment
rehistradot - registrar
rehistro - register, record
rekluta - recruit (soldier)
rekoha - to pluck or gather
rekohido - retired or frugal
rekomendasion - recommendation
rekomienda - to recommend
rekompensa - to recompense
rekonose - to recognize
rektifika - to rectify
rekuetda - to remind
relikias - relics
relos - watch, clock
reseta - prescription, recipe
resetba - to reserve, retain
resibe - to receive
residensia - residence
resiste - to disagree, contradict
resistensia - resistance
resolusion - resolution
respeta - to respect
respetao - respectful, polite
respekto - respect, reverence
responde - to respond
responsable - responsible
resutta - to result
retasos - shred
retira - to retire
retirao gi pumalo - isolated, secluded
retiro - seclusion
retorika - rhetoric
retrakta - to retract
reuma, mamuten tataotao - rheumatism
reunion - reunion
reusa - to decline, refuse
reyena - to replenish
ribana - to peel, pare, or cut away
ribat - rival, competitor

rienda - bridle, rein
riesgo - to risk, venture
rifa - raffle, lottery
riko - rich
riko na taotao - rich person
rinkon - corner, edge
rinesibe - receipt, acceptance
rineusa - depression of spirits
ripiti - repeat
ripoyu - cabbage
risibi - receive
riso i layak - to reef the sails
riyeno - wadding
roble - oak
robusto - robust, vigorous
rosa - rose
royo - roll
royon-tale - coil, coiled rope
rubentasion - deep sea
rueda - wheel
rumbo - route, course
rukkio' - pickled onion
rumot - rumor

sa' - due to the fact/because
sabalu - Saturday
sabana, ogso - hill, mountain
sabanas - bed sheets
sabio - sly, wise
sable - sword
sabot - flavor
saddok - river
sadi-gane - hut, shack
safe - to brush
saga - to stay, remain
sagamai - gnat, tiny insect
sagamelong - rose-colored squirrelfish
sagan - place, location
sagan amot - pharmacy
sagan benta - grocery
sagan famagu'on - nursery
sagan ga'ga' - stables
sagan hanom, tinaham hanom - water reservoir

sagan obeha - apiary

sagan paharo - aviarysagane - to guard

sagat - insolent

sagayan - place

sagayan na mayuti - lonely, deserted

sagaye - to settle down, colonize, occupy

sagrado - sacred

sagsag - red-colored, edible fish

sagua' - channel

sague - to pull or to guard

sa hafa, hafa taimano - why, to what extent

sahago, tadung na hanom - deep water

sahang - to shelve

sahgan - to case

sahgane - to fill or replenish

sahnge - distinct, special

sahyan, batko - ship

sahyau - quick, speedy

Saina - Lord

sais - six

sais sientos - six hundred

saka - to liberate

sakan - ripe, harvest

sakapiko - hatchet, axe

sake' - to steal, rob, or a thief

sako - coat

sakrifika - to sacrifice

sakrilego - sacrilegious

sakude - to shake

sala - hall or to disapprove

salamanka - to play tricks, trickster

salape' - money

salero - salt cellar

salida - departure

saligao - centipede

salinas - salt-making plant

salmon, satmon - salmon

salon - parlor

salud, hinemlo - health

saluda - to greet, salute

saludapble - wholesome, sound

salungai, bayena - whale

sandalias - sandals

sangan - to say, elect, appoint, name
sangan desparate - to swear under oath
sanganen patgon - to insinuate
sanganiye - to interpret, translate
sangano, desareglao - dissolute
san halom - inside, within
san hilo - on, upon, on top of
san hiyong - outward, without, outside
san lago - north
san lichan - west
san mena - in front, before, forward!
(i) sanmena - front
sano - healthy
san papa - below, underneath
san tati - rear, behind
Santo Espiritu - Holy Spirit
sanyeye - spider
saonao puminite - to express sympathy
saosao - to wipe
sapatos - shoes
sape'! - go away! (animals)
sapet - to torment
sapet maolek - to whip thoroughly
sapisapi - kite, or a type of colorful fish
sapit - to mortify, humble
sarangola - type of kite
sasahnge - devoid of inhabitants
sasalaguan, tinaifondo, infietno - hell, abyss
sasanganña - mode of speech
sasata - wasp
Sasatba - Savior
sasengat - a micronesian megapode (bird)
sastre - tailor
satanas, manganiti - satan, devil
satbabida - life boat
satge - floor, stage, platform
satira - satire, sarcasm
satisfecho - satisfied
satmon - salmon
satmoneti - red snapper
satna - itch or scab
satpa - to burn or squander
satsa - ketchup or sauce

saulak - to beat or whip
sebada - millet, barley
sebo, mantika - fat, lard
seboyas - onions
seda - silk
sede - to relent, yield
sedula, papeleta - ticket
segidiyas - a type of winged bean
segundo - second
seguro - sure or secure from danger
sehas - eyebrows
sekante - blotter
sekreto - secret
semana - week
Semanan Pasion - Passion Week, Holy Week
sementerero, lanchero - farmer, peasant
sementeyo - cemetery
semento - cement
semiya - seed, kernel
semnap - sunshine
sena - dinner
señas - to signal or a token
señat - symptom, sign
sendalo - soldier
sendalon kinababayo - cavalry soldier
sendangkulo' - enormous, excessive
senedot, sintoron, koreas - belt (waist)
senhuto, mahuto - exhausted, at the end
senisa - ashes, cinders
senmagahit - in all seriousness, certainly
señora - lady
señorita - young lady, single lady
señot - gentleman
senpoddong - to flunk or fail completely
sensen, katne - meat
sensiyo - simpleton
sentensia, huisio - sentence, judgment
sentensiadot - umpire
sentido, hinasso - mind, intellect
sentimentat - sentimental, romantic
sentimiento, siente - regret, feeling, sorrow
sentinela - guard
sentura - waist

separa - to separate
separasion - division
septiembre - September
sera - beeswax
seradura, kastiyo - citadel, castle
seremonias-gumayu'us - liturgy, ritual for public worship
serenata - serenade, evening music
sero - sero
serpiente, kulepbla - serpent, snake
sese - knife, or to stab
sesenta - sixty
sesiok - red squirrelfish
sesion - session
seso - often, frequent
se'so - separating coconut meat from the shell
sesonyan - marsh, bog
sesuye - to repeat, reiterate
sesyon - adult rabbitfish
setbe - useful
setbe hafa na empleo - to administer
setbesa - beer
setbiente, kriado - servant
setbisio - service
setbiyetas - napkins
setenta - seventy
setesientos - seven hundred
setmon - sermon
setro - scepter
seyo - seal, stamp
sibo - middle
siempre - always
siempre biba - life plant
siempre fiho - constant
sien - hundred
siente - to feel
siesta - nap
siete - seven
sietto - in truth, certain
siglo - century
sige - to follow or continue
sige' mona! adelanta - advance
siing - to push, crowd
sihig - terrestrial kingfisher

silaba - syllable
silindro - cylinder
simetrikat, man adanche - symmetrical
simiento - foundation
simple - simple
sin - zinc
sin - without
siña - to be able
sinague - protection, guard
siñaha - perhaps
sinahnge, retiro - seclusion
siña ma alado, aladuyon - arable, fit for plowing
siña maya, mamaya - navigable
sinangan, kuentos - statement, narrative, to quote
sinapet - torture, agony (mental or physical)
sinasalaguan - hellish, infernal, fiendish
siñat - type, sign
sinatisecho - satisfaction
sinaulak - sound beating
sin chumocho, fotmat - sober, earnest
singko - five
sinkuenta - fifty
sineguro - guarantee, pledge
sin enao - not withstanding
sinese, tinekcha, diniluk - stab or thrust
sinesede, kaso, inariesga - occurrence, event
sineso - copra
sinetsot, kontrision - contrition
siniabe, minanso - gentleness
sinibe - improvement
siniente - feeling, perception, sense of touch
siniso - shoot up or sprout
sinison chotda - young banana
siniye - to hold within
siniye, ulat - to hold within
sin medida - immoderation
sin moderasion - intemperance
sin na'an - nameless
sinonimo - synonym
sin parat - unbroken, without end
sin probecho - futile
sinta - edging, border
sikiera - at least

sirena - mermaid, siren
sise, titek - to rip or tear
sisiguiha, usune - to persist
sisiña - jurisdiction
sisi'ok - squirrelfish
sisoda - finder, one who finds
sisonyan - pool, puddle
sistema - system
sistematiko - systematic
sisuma - adder, viper
sitkulo - circle
sitio - courtyard, yard
siuda - city
siya - chair
siyan gaikanai - armchair
siyan machucan - rocking chair
sobetbio - proud
sobla - to remain
sobre kama - quilt, bedspread
sobren katta - envelope
sobresaliente - exceptional
sobretodo, manto - overcoat
sobrina - niece
sobrino - nephew
soda - to earn, acquire
sogne, hogse faaila - to accuse or charge someone with something
sogsog - consumptive
sokai - to tear
sokore, asiste, ayuda - to help
solamente - merely, only
solamente ke - unless
solemne - solemn
solo - isolated
sombra - shade, shaded area
somnak - sunny
somnap - sunlight
songge - inflamed, to burn up
songgiyon, gusi hanon, gusi mañila - inflammable
songsong - borough, village
sonido - tone, sound
sopas - soup
sopla - to blow away
soroho - bolt, door lock, to bolt the door

soso - to detach
sospecha - to suspicion
sospechoso - suspicious
sostiene - to sustain
sotana - robe
sotda - to solder
sotne - to stew, boil
sotse - to mend
sotta, dispensa, asii, na para - to forego
sottaye - to relax
sottera - maiden, unmarried woman
sottero - bachelor, unmarried
soyo, kombida, huho, ofrese, na osgon - to bid, persuade
suabe - suave
suabe na manglo - wind
sube - to promote, further
subida, chihit, humihot - approach, to draw nearer
submarino - submarine
subsigiente, tumatate - subsequently, later
suegra - mother-in-law
suegro - father-in-law
suelas, fangachaan, fefege, gacha - sole (foot)
suetdo - wage, payment
suette - luck, lucky
suetto - free
sufan - to pare
sugon - to frighten
sugun - to drive
suha! - away!
suhaye - to avoid
suheta - to repress
suheto - subject
suheto, mindiye, limitasion - restriction
sulon - to slide, slip
suma - to sum up
sumagagaye, okupante - occupant
sumai - to soak, wet
sumahnge, sumuha, mama tate - to straggle
sumanhiyong - exterior
sume - to leak through
sumegugundo - in second place
sumisiha - simultaneous
sumuspiros - to sob, sigh with tears

suncho - hoop, metal or wooden band
sungon - to forbear, patient
suni - taro
suog - to induce, persuade
suon - to elate, raise one's spirits
suplente - vicarious
suplika - to beg
supone - to suppose
supuk, lumus - to submerge in water
susede - to befall or happen
suseso - success
susonyan - swamp
suspiros - to lament, complain, sigh
sustansia - being, matter, substance
sustento, nengkanno lina'la - substinence, livelihood
susu - breast (female)
sutko, kanat, hoya, hoyo – furrow

tabetna - inn, tavern
tabla - board, table
tablon - plank
tacho - to stand up, get up
tacho - perpendicular
tachong gi halom guma Yu'us - pew
tachong ni taiapo - seat, chair
tadung - large, deep
tadung na hanom - deep water
taftaf - early
tagahilo - grand
tago - to command
tagmomye - quarrelsome
tagpange - to baptize
tagpapa - reptile
tagpapaña - subordinate
taguan - to entrust
tai- - without
taiachaigua - superior
taiadotno - simple
taialentos - breathless
taiase - savage, brutal
taiatension - impolite, boorish
taibale - worthless, frivolity
taibale na taotao - wretch, worthless person

taibisio - virtuous
taichecho - idleness
taichetnot - uninjured
taichi - limitless, immense
taichilong - matchless, peerless
taikumalanten - constant
taiesperensia - inexperienced
taifinakpo - endless
taifinaitai - imperishable
taigachong - odd person
taiganas - without appetite
taigasto - cheap
taigrasia - farce
taiguailaye - unfit, in vain
taigue - absent
taiguihi - such, the same as
taiginalamten - unchanging
taiha'ane - lifeless, dead
taihinasso - ignorant
taihinekok - everlasting
taiinadahe - recklessness
taiinangoko - independent
taiinina - not showy
taiinteres - unbiased
taiisao - innocent, not guilty
tailaye - evil, vulgar
tailinache - infallable, unerring
taima'añao - courageous, bold, audacious, fearless
taimaestima, taipresio - priceless, incalculable
taimahgong - troublesome
taimamahlao - shameless, insolent
taimancha - unstained
taimanglo - no wind
taiminagof, malagana - sad, full of grief, disappointment
taiminangi - distasteful
taiminaolek - sterile, barren
taimineton - fickleness
taininangga - hopeless, desperate
taioson - patient
taipareho - highest degree, utmost
taipasensia,tenhos - impatient
taipeligro - safe
taipresio - priceless

taipunta, obtuso, ñaño, foda - obtuse
tairemedio - incurable
tairespeto - disrespectful
taisabot - tasteless
taisaga - needy, indigent
taisakan - no harvest
taisalape - poor
taiseguro - unsafe
taisentido - moron
taisetbe - rudeness
taisinahguan - empty
taisinatesfecho - insatiable
taisinetsot - impenitence
taisiniente - senseless
taitai - to read
taitano - landless
taitingfong - nothing to count
taitiningo - devoid of reason
tahgue - to take the place of
tahlang - to weigh by hand
tahlek - twist
taka - to reach
take - feces
take ga'ga' - animal excrement
take lulok - rust
takon - heel
takuri - kettle
tala - to expose
talaktak - noise, bang
talai - to level to the ground
talanga - ear
talanga hayo - mushroom, sponge
talangan hulo - thunder
talapos - rag
talaya - net
talayero, peskadot - fisherman
tale - rope, string, line
talen atgoya - guide line for carabao
Talo - Equator, center
ta'lo - again
taloane - noon
ta'lo tate - to recall
talon humaso - to return to one's mind

taluye - to lengthen
tamaño - immense
tambot - drum
tampat - flounder
tampe - to cover, a cover or lid
tampoko - neither
tamtam - to sample food
tancho - to show
tane - to entertain
tane' - to try food
tanga - deaf
tankat - cage
tangkala - porous
tangse - to mourn
tangsiyon - pitiful
tangis - to cry, howl
tanke - tank
tanme, chetnot - infection
tano, oda - land
i tano, mundo - the world
tano maipe - the tropics
tantea - to feel
tanto - so much
tanto___komo___ - ___as well as
tanum - to sow, plant
taotao - person, man
taotao huyong - foreign-born resident
taotao lago - European
taotao ni man mamomokkat - pedestrian
taotao siha - inhabitants
tapis - apron
taplung - to repeat
tarakito - pompano fish
tarea - homework, chores
tarifa - tariff
tarheta - card
tasa - cup, saucer
tasa - to appreciate
tasi - sea, ocean
tasme - to sharpen (i.e. pencil)
tasyon - wet
tat, nunka - never
tata - father

tataka - sentimental
tataka - to seek blindly
ta'ta'ga - a type of black fish
tatago - magistrate
tatalo - back
tatalo puenge - midnight
tatalun - a type of brown fish
tatamung - a type of fish with black and yellow coloring
tatancho - forefinger
tatane - glamour, fascination
tataotao - human body
tatate - progeny
tatate matai - to survive
tatatse - poisonous
tate - rear
tate - to follow
taten - in rear of
taten ogso - mountainside
tatnai mayuma, bithen - virgin, maiden
tatne - to bury or entomb
tatnero - calf
tatnon - to recover
tatse - poison
tattamudo - stutterer or stammerer
tauhan - inflammation
taya - nothing, zero
taya nai - never, nowhere
taya sebla - there's nothing left
tayok - jump
tayogue - to leap
tayuyut - to beg
techa - prayer leader
techo - roof (house)
tegcha - fruitful
tegcho - carnivorous
tegpong - floor
teha - tile, brick
tekon - to bend down or take down
telefono - telephone
telegragia de radio - radio telegraph
telegrama - telegram
telipas goma para hanom - rubber hose (water)
temperaturan tano - climate

templa - to thin
templao - mixed
templansa - temperance
templo - temple
tenasa - tongs
tenda - store
tendero - storekeeper
tenedot - fork
tenedot basula - pitchfork
tenedot i lepblo - bookkeeper
tentago - subject, one under control of another
tentasion - temptation
teok - thick
tesgue - to steal or cheat
tesna - fog or soot
tesorero - treasurer
testamento - testament
testigo - witness, jury
testiguye - to testify
testimonio - testimony
tetmina - to terminate
tetminao para ayo finataiña - fatal
tetmino - brief period
tetmometro - thermometer
tetsiopelo - velvet
tia - aunt
ti abag - not mistaken
ti abmam - forthwith, recent
ti akomparayon - incomparable
ti animoso - discouraged
tiao - a type of silvery fish
ti apattayon - indivisible
ti areglao - irregular
ti astiyon - inexcusable
ti atanon - horrid
ti bibubo - patient
ti chatao - unselfish
ti chuma'on - incorrigible
ti dadage - truthful
ti dinanche - incorrect
ti ebitayon - imperative
tiempo - weather
tiempon ayunat - fasting time, Lent, Shrovetide

i tiempo ni mapos - past, the time gone by
tiempon maipe - summer
tiempon manengheng - winter
tienda i kampaña - tent
tienta - to try
ti esplikayon - inexplicable
ti estotbayon - cool, calm
ti fafababa - loyal, faithful
ti fafañago - barren, unfruitful
ti fafanokcha - barren
ti fahateg, fatinason - possible
ti fiet - infidel, unfaithful
ti fiho - vague, indefinite, unsettled
ti fiho hinasoña - unstable, changeable
ti finababa - allegiance (to a country)
ti gobietnayon - unruly, turbulent, ungovernable
tiguaguan - cheap
ti guailaye - immaterial, unessential
ti guaiyayon - hateful
ti gefhomhom - melancholy
ti gefmunhayan - incomplete
ti igiyon - limitless
ti hasuyon - unaccountable for
ti hatraidute - faithful, loyal
ti hengge - infidel, ungodly, unbelieving
tiheras - scissors
tiheras guma - rafters
ti hihikok - eternal
ti honggiyon - incredible
ti hulaton - invincible, unconquerable
ti komprendiyon - to gibber
ti kontento - discounted
ti kabales - imperfect
ti kahulo - to fail
ti lahi ni ti palao'an - neuter (either sex)
ti lalache, estrikto - accurate, precise
ti liion - imperceptible, not easily grasped by the mind
ti lilisto - unprepared, not ready
tilipas - intestines
ti maangoko - distrusted, doubted, suspected
ti magahit - unreal, false
ti magas - inferior
ti magof - disappointed, gloomy

ti magof tataotao - dizzy, giddy
ti ma guiaiya - odious, unpopular
ti mahahaga - not bloody
ti mahasngon - accidentally, casually
ti malague, aguaguat - to disagree
timalango - healthy (body)
timamahñao, matatnga, mamalahi - manly, courageous
ti manananga - natural, accidental
ti manangga - casual
ti manangoke - to despair
ti mañieñiente - numb, torpid
ti manhongge - wicked
ti manmerese - unworthy
ti mangge - unsavory
ti mannggi - tasteless
ti manpareho - several, various, different
ti maog - fleeting, in transition
ti mapot - easy, not difficult
ti masa - uncooked
ti ma tetmina - indeterminate
ti maolek - evil, ill, sick, diseased
ti mesngon - peevish
ti meton hinasoña - unsteady, unreliable
timinalago - objection
timon - helm, rudder
timonero - steersman
timunok tilipas - rupture
tinadong - depth
tinaemaolek - malice
tinaga - cut
tinago, mision, finamaolek -mission, order
tinakpange - baptism
tinaiboluntad - ill will
tinaichi - eternity
tinaichii - to enhance
tinaidakon, tinaidinagi - truthfulness
tinaifondo - hell
ti naimalofan - impassable
tinaigue - absence
tinaihinasso - ignorance
tinaipeligro - free from danger
tinaisetbe - disability
tinaitai - prayer

tinaitai hinalom - silent prayer (inwards)
tinaha - old earthen crock or pitcher
tinahan hanom - water reservoir
tinake - rusty
tinalo - central
ti namalango - hygienic, sanitary
tinane - occupation
tinanga - deafness, wish
ti nangayun - improbable
tinanum - plantation
tinanum ubas - vineyard
tina para umo'mak - bathtub
tinasa - pliers
i tinateña - third, next
tinekcha - berry
tinemba, tinigua - depression
tinempla - moderation
tinemton - talent, mental capacity
ti ngangason - indigestible
tinienta, tentasion - temptation
tinifok - webbing
tinifok gapanulo yan lana - felt, wool fabric
tinifong - accounting
tinige kannai - handwriting
tinilaika - alteration, mutation
tinina, bendision - praise
tininas - honesty, justification
tiningo - wisdom, knowledge
tininon somnap - sunburned
tinito - shelled rice, ground coffee
i tinituhon - germ, organism
tinta - ink
tintero - inkstand
tio - uncle
tipadok, ñahlalang - thrifty
ti parayon hanonña - inextinguishable
ti pareho - dissimilar
ti preparao - unprepared
ti propio - improper, erroneous
tira - to shoot
tirano - oppressive
tirante - suspenders
tirarañas - cobwebs

tiro - shot
ti sasakan - immature, unripe
ti seguro - unsafe
ti seso - rare, remarkable
tiso - rigid, inflexible
tiso na pulo - stiff hair
ti sumiña - to render unfit
ti sungunon - intolerable
ti takaon, chomchom, ti hatmiyon - inpenetrable
titanos - brain, marrow
titek - to rip or tear
titienta - tempter
ti tinaka - insufficient
titires - buffoon
titiyas - tortillas
titokcha - bee sting
ti tratusan - stubborn
tituka - thistle, thorn
titufok - weaver
ti tufungon - countless
tituge', eskrebiente - writer, clerk
ti tulakayon - immutable
ti tunas - indirect, not straightforward
ti tungon na minagahet - secret
ti yamakon - indesctructable
ti yayayas - undefeatable
ti yodahe - carelessness, reckless, loitering
toa, sakan, masa - ripe, ready for harvest
toaya - towel
tochong - to knot, a knot
todo – everything, all
todohanasiña – Almighty
todos mangigigoha – altogether
tokcha – to ram
toke – stroke
tokpong – handle
toktok – hug
toktok duro – to cling
tohe – to drip
tohge – stand
tohne – to support
tola – refuse, to spit out
tolang – bone

tolang espinaso - vertebra
tolang kaderas – hip bone
tolang kiadas – jawbone
tolompo – top (toy), to play
tomates – tomatoes
tomo – knee, volume
tomon kannai – elbow
tompo – trip
tomtom – wise, sensible, crafty
tomtom gi tiningo – scientific
tonada – tune
tongho – neck
tongtong – to strike, thrust
tonto – silly, stupid
tore – tower
torete – steer
toriyo – a type of fish
toro – bull
toron binadu – stag, male deer
tosino – pork
tosta – toast, or burned
totche – to splice
totmento – to splice
totmento – torment
totnge – screw
totno – lathe
totno – to turn on a lathe
toto – to root out
totot – turtledove
totpe – collision
totpe – to nudge
totpedo – torpedo
toyo – to wince
traban chachak – saw set
trabia – not yet
traduse – to interpret
traidot – faithless
traidute – to betray
traison – imposition
trahe – frock
trampas – trick, lie, swindle
tramposo – swindler, rogue
tranka – to bolt the door

tranka – gate, gateway
trankan potta – door latch
trankilo – tranquil
trapiche – sugar mill
traslada – removal, transfer
traslada – to translate
trasplanta – to transplant
traspotta – to transport
traskila – to shave
trastes biahe – traveling
trastes gerra – armament
trastes halom guma – furniture
trata – to treat
trates – implement
trates guma – house furnishings
tratos – to traffic, proceedings, relations
tratos pot kometsio – to negotiate
treinta – thirty
tres – three
trese – thirteen
tresientos – three hundred
triangolo – triangle
tribunat – tribunal, court
tribute todo, impuesto, katga – duty, tax
trigo – wheat, grain
trinaidot – treason
trinaidute – treason, treachery
trinamposo – swindling, cheating
trinchera – trench, excavation
Trinidad – Holy Trinity
trireste – very sorrowful, grieving
trompeta – trumpet
trongko – tree, trunk
trongkon familia – family tree
trongkon hanom – fountain or spring
trongkon hayo – tree trunk
troson lamlam – thunderbolt
tuba – palm wine
tuban kandet – lamp shade
tubatuba – physic nut
tubo – tube
tubon piao – reed pipe, bamboo pipe
tuka – to tease, vex, penetrate, hint

tucho – to consume (also a word for "checkmate")
tufok – to weave
tufong – to count
tugong – to charge, attack, or take hold of
tugua – to pull down
tuge – to write
tuhong – hat, bonnet
tuhus – to satiate
tulaika – to exchange
tulisan, bandolero – bandit
tumachu – upright, vertical
tumada – dose (medication)
tumalo – to return
tumatate – later
tumattamudo – to stutter
tumaya – to dispense
tumo – to tan leather, dye
tumola – to spit
tumu – to dye
tumunok – to descend
tumunok tilipas – unbiased, indifferent
tuna – to praise
tunan maisa – to praise
tunas – lawful, honest
tunas hulo an papa – upright
tunas na tiningo – morality, ethics
tunayon – praiseworthy
tungo – to comprehend
tunguon – intelligible
tuniko – garment, tunic
tunok – to step down
tupak – fishing line
tupat – sling
tupo – well
tupo – sugar cane
tutbio – foggy, misty, cloudy
tuto – to trample
tutu – to pound, to grind
tutuhon – origin, beginning, to commence
tuyan – stomach, abdomen
ubas - grapes
uchaga lahe – spike rush (plant)
uchan – rain

udo - dumb
uko – to hum
ufa – looking-glass tree
uga – to flatter
ugis – gray
ugupa amariyo – a type of colorful fish
uhang - shrimp
ulen – to steer a vessel
ulo – head
ulu – caterpillar
uma – together, opposite each other
umaatok – snug, concealed
umakamo – wedlock
umachaigua, aparente, pumarereho – apparent
umacheton – to join or unite
umacheton – closely connected
umachuli – mutual
umachuli, chinichili – looking alike
umakontratta – to bind by contract
umadespatta – asunder
umadisepatta, famokkat – to depart, move, leave
umafababa – to cheat each other
umagang – to exclaim suddenly
umagang mamatai – clamor
umagonias – to be in the last throes of death
umaguaguat – quarrel
umaguesgues – friction
umahoye – to enter into an agreement
umanidad – humanity
umapayune – familiar
umasagua – to marry
umasaguan malago – to elope
umaso – to sag or sink down
umatane – entertainment
umatattiye – consecutive
umatok – to steal away
umatotpe – to collide
umatratos – to come to an understanding
umatungong – to encounter
umatungo – to agree
umaya – to be alike
umaya – accurate, exact
umayuti, dibutsia – to divorce

umekakat – gingerly
umechino – to play the mendicant
umegagao – to beg
i umegagao limosna – beggar
umentalo – to interfere
umeskapa – to steal away
umesalao – shouting
umido – humid, moist
umisao – to sin
umitdat, inimitde – humility
umitde – meek
umiya – to humiliate
umok – yard grass
umudo – to become silent
umugong – to groan, lament
unai – sand
uniko, mamaisa ha – unique
unifotme – unifrm
unhanao! – be gone !
uno – one
unoha – single, only one
upos – to exceed
upu – to take off the top
upus – gone by
usa – to use
usao – used, worn
uso – wear, use
usun – to lie down
usune – to persist
utsa – to careen
uttimo, finakpo – ultimate, utmost
uttimon minagof – rapture
utut – to cut
u'uchan – raining
uyu – a certain person

ya - and, so
yabalak - to tear to pieces
yabao - to reap
yabe - key
ya-hu - I like, I love
yahulolo - above all, upper side
yaka - to crumple up

yalibao - to brandish
yamak - to fracture, break
ya-mu - you like, you love
yan - and, versus
yaña - he/she likes/loves
yanggin - if, whenever
yan-miyu - you like/love
yano - level, plain, even
yan-ñiha - they like/love
yanta - tire (wheel)
yanto - wail, moan
yapapapa - base, foundation
yaya - to shatter
yayaguag - nest swift
yayas - to be tired, fatigued
yedra - ivy
yelmon - helmet
yema - yolk of an egg
yengyong, chalauchau - earthquake
yeno - full, replete
yeso - plaster, chalk
yetna - daughter-in-law
yetno - son-in-law
yinalaka - mutation, variation
yinauyau - din, deafening noise
yinease - charity
yinemok - vengeance, revenge
yinengyong - movement
yinilang - devestation caused by a storm
yiniti - divorce
yiniusan - solemn, serious
yo'ase - gracious, good, merciful
yodahe - solicitous
yogua - to discard
yomahlo, machalek - shy, timid
yomok - fat, fleshy
yu - I, me
yugo - yoke
yulang - to break, destory, annihilate
yuma - to touch
yuti - to cast away, to throw
yuti papa - to degrade, lower physically
Yu'us - God

References

- Cunningham, Lawrence (1992). *Ancient Chamorro Society.* Honolulu, Hawaii: Bess Press,
- Farrell, D. (1991). History of the Northern Mariana Islands. Saipan, CNMI: Public School System, Commonwealth of the Northern Mariana Islands.
- Topping, Donald M., Pedro Ogo, and Bernadita Dungca (1975). *Chamorro-English Dictionary.* Honolulu: University Press of Hawaii.
- Topping, Donald M., Pedro Ogo, and Bernadita Dungca (1973). *Chamorro-Reference Grammar.* Honolulu: University Press of Hawaii.
- Topping, Donald M., Pedro Ogo, and Bernadita Dungca (1980). Spoken *Chamorro.* Honolulu: University Press of Hawaii.
- von Preissig, E. R. (1918). *Dictionary and Grammar of the Chamorro Language of the Island of Guam.* Washington DC: Department of the Navy: Govt. print. off.

Acknowledgements

This book would not have been possible without my mother, Teresita Santos Brookfield of San Roque, Saipan. Without her wit, wisdom, and tough Chamorro love, I wouldn't be the stubborn, ambitious Chamaole that I am today. I love you and hope to always make you proud.

ABOUT THE AUTHOR

M.B. Dallocchio is a Chamorro artist and author who served as a medic, mental health sergeant, and retention NCO in the US Army for eight years. While on deployment to Ramadi, Iraq in 2004-2005, she served as a member of "Team Lioness," the first female team that was attached to Marine infantry units to perform checkpoint operations, house raids, and personnel searches on Iraqi women and children for weapons and explosives.

After her return in 2006, she pursued studies in international relations as a David L. Boren National Security Education Program language scholar in Europe. At the same time, noticing a need within the Chamorro community, she created the Chamorro Language and Culture blog to aid others in learning the Chamorro language and maintaining Chamorro traditions.

She was featured in the 2008 documentary film "Lioness," a PBS documentary entitled "The Long Road Home," and several books covering women in combat and racial injustice. In 2009, she was awarded the Outstanding Woman Veteran Award by the State of Massachusetts for her service in both the military and the veteran community.

Dallocchio is the author of "Quixote in Ramadi: An Indigenous Account of Imperialism" as well as the Women Warriors chapter of the book, "War Trauma and Its Wake." She has been featured in the San Francisco Chronicle, Huffington Post, Las Vegas Review-Journal, PBS, Yahoo! News, and many other media outlets covering facing injustice during and after combat. Dallocchio also speaks out on indigenous rights, imperialism, gender equality, and the importance of self-empowerment.

She currently resides in Las Vegas, Nevada with her spouse and two children.

For more information about M.B. Dallocchio, visit:
www.thedesertwarrior.com

Made in the USA
Middletown, DE
10 August 2022